DIS Her war

♦

American Women in WWII

*Edited by
Kathryn S Dobie and Eleanor Lang*

iUniverse, Inc.
New York Lincoln Shanghai

Her War
American Women in WWII

All Rights Reserved © 2003 by Kathryn Dobie

No part of this book may be reproduced or transmitted in any form or by any means, graphic, electronic, or mechanical, including photocopying, recording, taping, or by any information storage retrieval system, without the written permission of the publisher.

iUniverse, Inc.

For information address:
iUniverse, Inc.
2021 Pine Lake Road, Suite 100
Lincoln, NE 68512
www.iuniverse.com

ISBN: 0-595-30373-0

Printed in the United States of America

For Al Dobie,

HER WAR's greatest supporter

Contents

PROLOGUE 1

CHAPTER 1   LEADERS AND ADVOCATES 3
- *OVETA CULP HOBBY 5*
- *MARY MCLEOD BETHUNE 7*
- *JOSEPHINE VON MIKLOS 9*
- *MARGARET HICKEY 12*

CHAPTER 2   FACTORY WORKERS 15
- *AUGUSTA CLAWSON 17*
- *CONSTANCE BOWMAN AND CLARA MARIE ALLEN 26*
- *JOSEPHINE VON MIKLOS 33*

CHAPTER 3   NURSES 41
- *HELEN MCKEE 43*
- *MARTA GORICK 50*
- *RUTH HASKELL 53*
- *JEAN TRUCKEY 59*
- *JUNE WANDREY 62*
- *JUANITA REDMOND 64*

CHAPTER 4   MILITARY AND ALLIED SERVICE
                 PERSONNEL 69
- *MARY-AGNES BROWN 72*
- *VERA HAMERSCHLAG 75*
- *DOROTHY SCHWARTZ 78*
- *LORENA HERMANCE 81*
- *CORNELIA FORT 89*

- *WASP* *92*

Chapter 5   CIVIL RIGHTS SUPPORTERS AT HOME 105
- *SONOKO IWATA AND MARY UYESAKA* *107*
- *MARY MCLEOD BETHUNE* *111*
- *WACs* *115*

Chapter 6   WAR CORRESPONDENTS 127
- *MARGARET BOURKE-WHITE* *129*
- *MARTHA GELLHORN* *139*
- *PATRICIA LOCHRIDGE* *152*

Chapter 7   CLANDESTINE ACTIVIST 158
- *MARGARET UTINSKY* *160*

EPILOGUE 181

PROLOGUE

For most citizens of the world, World War II was a clearly defined struggle between good and evil. The militant nationalism and racism which characterized the totalitarian government of Germany were recognized and feared throughout the human community. As Germany advanced through Europe, independent governments were deprived of their sovereignty and their citizens were stripped of their personal freedom. These acts of aggression would eventually culminate in acts of savagery which still stun people today.

A policy of appeasement kept France and Great Britain from declaring war on Germany until its armed forces overran Poland in September of 1940, while Americans debated the wisdom of direct involvement. The United States sold, loaned, or leased supplies to the defenders of Europe, but resisted being drawn into the conflict.

The imperialist government of Japan, dominated by the military, had already begun its intended expansion into the Far East with invasions into Manchuria and sections of China. The national slogan, "Hakko Ichiu", "Bringing the Eight Corners of the World Under One Roof", proclaimed their intentions. Although the United States also sold defense materials to China, that war, so distant from America's shores, seemed irrelevant to Americans and to their friends in Europe. The United States' policy of nonintervention came to an abrupt end with the brutal Japanese attack on the unsuspecting American forces at Pearl Harbor on December 7, 1941.

On December 8, the United States formally declared war on Japan. Three days later, Germany and Italy added the United States to their list of avowed enemies. The United States would fight on two fronts against forces threatening liberty and democracy. The Allied powers and the ideals they espoused would prevail, but the sacrifices required would be enormous. Only an evil of such staggering scope could have fostered the commitment and sustained the sacrifices made by the servicemen of the United States, with their allies, to this cause.

There are still names of battles that conjure up visions of courage and endurance, sacrifice and heroism, for today's American citizens: Iwo Jima, the Bataan Death March, Normandy, the Battle of the Bulge. It is natural and fitting for the country to remember and memorialize the conflicts of banner headlines, the well-chronicled exploits of men who fought and suffered, endured or died.

But numerous contributions to World War II have gone unheralded. These largely unknown achievements were the work of groups whose role was to support and sustain the conflict. Many of these heroes were women who relinquished the security of home and time-honored roles to face the unknown in answer to the nation's call. As the need for men in the armed services escalated, a crescendo of voices, including those of public women, urged women to support these men by producing planes, ships, and ammunition, by attending the ill and wounded, by filling jobs in the military vacated by men called up for active duty. They could and they did. Other women interpreted the call for women's help by acting as war correspondents to keep U.S. citizens informed, while a few worked in secret, aiding prisoners of the Japanese or servicemen caught behind enemy lines. Most of these women suffered deprivation and loss; many faced the threat of death. All these women became vital components in the all-encompassing life-and-death struggle to defeat Germany and Japan and preserve liberty and democratic ideals.

Different women from different walks of life were part of this freedom offensive; only those who wrote personal accounts of their war experiences at the time are represented here. Many of these women wrote home to loved ones, sharing their anxieties and triumphs; some committed their experiences to personal journals; still others wrote speeches and articles, or autobiographies, intended for the general reading public. All of these accounts exemplify the generous response, the tremendous commitment and valuable service American women gave to the cause of freedom during World War II. One designer turned factory worker expressed a consciousness many women shared:

> After all, the crux of the matter is that there is a job to be done to which we have been called. It is a job that must be done and there seems to be no two ways about it. It must be done even if it is a hard job, sometimes unpleasant, often a little beyond the limit of our strength. But it seems to be a fact—to vary Alice Through the Looking Glass—that if we do only as much as we can, we won't get much beyond the point where we started. It is the extra ounce of strength, the extra bit of strain, and, perhaps most of all, the last particle of enthusiasm which will finish the job.
>
> —Von Miklos

This is the story of *Her War*.

1

LEADERS AND ADVOCATES

After the United States was catapulted into World War II with the attack on Pearl Harbor, the rapid mobilization of the military and the expansion of wartime industries created an unprecedented number of jobs. The male population alone could not satisfy the demands of a country at war, and the need for women's work was recognized.

From this crisis women leaders quickly emerged. These women assumed two responsibilities: to organize all those women who were eager to volunteer their services and to convince others that their skills and their talents were essential to winning the war.

The most prominent of these leaders were those who took command of the women's sections of the Army, Navy, Marine Corps and Coast Guard. Never before had so many women—400,000—been associated with the military and never before had the opportunity to serve as officers presented itself. Oveta Culp Hobby, for example, was asked to guide the newly created Women's Army Auxiliary Corps. When she addressed its first officer candidate class, she shared with her WAACs the historic implications of that moment when "established precedents of military tradition [gave] way to pressing need."

Mary McLeod Bethune, a long time advocate for African Americans' rights and president of the National Council of Negro Women, urged her membership to support the war effort with total commitment. Dedication and sacrifice were required of every American, even those who had not fully participated in its benefits, if the democratic ideals of America were to be preserved.

> Beware of the subversive influences which may try to beguile you into thinking that we have not played a big part in the making of this country, and that it is not ours to defend. For America is our home. We have fought for her in every battle, we have worked for her, we are willing to walk the last mile in defending her.

Austrian visitor Josephine Von Miklos came to America expecting to discover a way of life inferior to the cultural standards of central Europe. Instead, she became enthralled with the character of American society and the attitude of its people, and she embraced what she came to identify as "this America of mine." Thirteen years later, when America was drawn into the conflict in Europe and Asia, she perceived the war as a threat to the democratic freedoms and American values she "had learned to love and cherish in [those] wonderful American years." "So there wasn't a shadow of a doubt in my mind that when the mess came to America, it meant me too."

Von Miklos fulfilled her personal pledge to defend the way of life she had come to prize by leaving her comfortable job in New York City to work first in a munitions factory and, later, in a shipyard. As she stated in her preface, Von Miklos wrote *I Took A War Job* in 1943 to "serve as something of a guide for those women who are coming and who will, in ever-increasing numbers, have to come into the world of the skilled worker. Maybe they will take heart if they are told, as I have tried to tell them, that this world is all right."

By 1944, even with millions of women in defense plants and hundreds of thousands in the military, still more were needed, not only in work directly related to the war, but in essential civilian trades and services. Crisscrossing the country, Margaret Hickey, chair of the Women's Advisory Committee of the War Manpower Commission, took responsibility for galvanizing those who had not yet volunteered. This war, she said, "will require the full utilization of America's total brain and brawn. This means that no individual can escape the war. Every woman, as well as every man, must respond to the necessity of this hour."

OVETA CULP HOBBY

In May of 1942, Representative Edith Nourse Rogers of Massachusetts introduced a bill, passed by Congress, which created an all volunteer women's corps attached to the Army. Oveta Culp Hobby, a civic and social activist from Houston, Texas, chosen as the first director, was disappointed that the women were to serve as auxiliaries to the Army, working with it but not in it. In the fall of 1943, this situation was rectified.

The following is an excerpt from an address by Hobby to the first class of women officer candidates who initiated a new tradition at Fort DesMoines, Iowa in July of 1943.

May 14th...President Roosevelt signed a bill...creating the Women's Army Auxiliary Corps.... It is a date that will grow in significance as this Corps fulfills its vital purpose....

Long established precedents of military tradition have given way to pressing need.... Women have long wanted to volunteer; now the need is here, and many have answered their country's call.

...This is <u>your</u> date with destiny, and a free future will credit your contribution. You are the first women to serve as an auxiliary force with the Army of the United States. Never forget it.

You have just made the change from peacetime pursuits to wartime tasks. From the individualism of civilian life to the anonymity of mass military life. You have given up comfortable homes, highly paid positions, leisure. You have taken off silk and put on khaki. And all for essentially the same reason—you have a debt and a date. A debt to democracy, a date with destiny.

You do not come into a Corps that has an established tradition. You must make your own. But in making your own, you do have one tradition—the integrity of all the brave American women of all time who have loved their country....

You, as you gather here, are living history. On your shoulders will rest the military reputation and the civilian recognition of this Women's Army Auxiliary Corps. I have reviewed the papers of every one of you. I have no fear that any woman here will fail the standards of this Corps.

From now on, you are soldiers, defending a free way of life. Your performance here, in the field, and abroad, will set the standards of the Corps. This is a hard task. You will live in the spotlight. Even though the lamps of experience are dim, few, if any, mistakes will be permitted you....

You will be called upon to give up most of the things you have enjoyed as individuals. You may be called upon to give your lives....

In the final analysis the only testament free people can give to the quality of freedom is the way they resist the forces that peril freedom. This Corps is a testament of free women defending a free way of life, to the exclusion of everything else, until the war against the Axis is won....

—Source: "Greetings to the Officer Candidates July 23, 1942" by Oveta Culp Hobby, Series 7, "Speeches, 1020–1983," Box 43, Folder 15, Oveta Culp Hobby Papers, 1817–1995, MS 459, Woodson Research Center, Fondren Library, Rice University.

MARY MCLEOD BETHUNE

The education, training and employment of African American women was the focus of Mary Bethune's life for thirty years. To accomplish her goals, she forged interracial political alliances. During World War II she worked closely with Oveta Culp Hobby, head of the Women's Army Corps, and with Franklin and Eleanor Roosevelt, and was appointed the federal government's Director of the Division of Negro Affairs. In this role she championed the integration of African American women both as officers and enlisted personnel in the armed forces and as trained workers in defense plants. In the following letter written as President of the National Council of Negro Women, she urges full participation by the membership in the war for democracy at home and overseas.

To the National Council of Negro Women:

I am happy to greet you in the spirit of our increased responsibilities. The year before us presents to our organization a challenge which we have never had to face before. In a world where hate, greed and fear are vying for upper-most position; where bitterness is striving to replace love, defeatism to replace hope, with prejudices running rampant, brother pitted against brother, and starvation and suffering on every side, we would be discouraged if we did not know that God still lives. We face these problems with the same spirit of understanding and sacrifice which has characterized the Negro woman in all ages, who trod the thorny road steadily and with utter confidence, leaving to us the greater heritage. As a significant part of the womanhood of all America, with characteristic fortitude and vision, we will shoulder our full share of responsibility.

These are stirring times! Our country is at war, and in order to help our country win the war we must realize the responsibility that rests upon each individual woman. In a spirit of loyalty and understanding, we will give the full extent of our strength toward the conservation of our hard-earned gains as a race, and toward the preservation of the ideals of democracy for every group in this country. It was for such a time as this that our Council was born. I am most anxious that each woman in our Council realize how much the times demand the fullest development and use of her potentialities.... Beware of subversive influences which may try to beguile you into thinking that we have not played a big part in the making of this country, and that it is not ours to defend. For America is our home. We have fought for her in every battle, we have worked for her, we are willing to walk the last mile in defending her....

The privilege has been given us to defend the essentials of human living set forth in our constitution, as life, liberty and the pursuit of happiness. Without these there can be no happiness for any one. This fact should stir every American, whether man, woman or child, to the utmost in sacrifice, action and vigilance. We dream of the great America of tomorrow to which we give in work today the "last full measure of devotion." May God sustain us now and in the years to come.

—Source: "The President's Message," by Mary McLeod Bethune, <u>The Aframerican Women's Journal</u>, Vol. II, Winter 1941–42, No. 3, National Council of Negro Women Collection, National Park Service—Mary McLeod Bethune Council House NHS, Washington, D.C.

JOSEPHINE VON MIKLOS

America was not always "home" for Josephine Von Miklos. Austrian by birth and a European by inclination, she had visited America rather tentatively, fully expecting to return home after sampling American culture. But she fell in love with the principles and the people—and stayed. "I have learned that there are a few things of permanent importance, things like freedom, warmth, understanding, courage, and integrity. And a real laugh. So there."

I came to America in 1930, when it was just a place one might visit, as one had visited many places before. I was born in Vienna, had left it to marry a Hungarian, and then, when that hadn't worked out, had spent a few years traveling over the map of Europe. New York was just another town to be looked at. English was just another language to be spoken, as one spoke several others, as a matter of course and education. I was pretty sure, then, that I wouldn't like America; how could I? They didn't know anything about culture in America, that culture which for so long had been the birthright of central European nations. I was dead certain, then, that America, amusing though it might be, would make me want to go back rather quickly to the ladylike behavior of the people who were my own kind, to the gentlemanly manners of the class to which I belonged.

Well, after I had got over the shock of Manhattan's skyline and of New York itself; after I had traversed the American continent in an old roadster, looking at America's cities and plains and rivers; after I had seen a Negro baptism in the Mississippi and Indian dances in New Mexico; after I had been stuck for two weeks in the rainy desert mud of Arizona and had looked at a movie set in Hollywood—I never went back, really back.

If I wanted to stay I had to start making a living for the first time in my life. I made it, although working on a daily professional basis was something very new to me. My family were well off when I was a child at home. Later my husband and his large estate had provided. But when I decided to stay in America he stopped the monthly allowance. He had an idea that he wasn't interested in supporting an estranged wife separated by an ocean; maybe I should have fought on the grounds that geography didn't have very much to do with legal arrangements. But I didn't fight or even argue. I decided that I had been a drone long enough. I decided that it was much more in keeping with the new lessons that this new land was teaching me to try to get used to the idea of getting along on my own hook. It wasn't easy, the first couple of years. In fact, it was pretty tough. But somehow it did work. Somehow I did get along. After a while it got to be all right.

I had had no friends in this strange country, but gradually I made better friends than I had ever made before. I had only the vaguest idea about the syntax of this language, but pretty soon the words came, the good long fancy words, the big American ten-dollar words, and the swell little ones, the bad ones, those that a lady doesn't use.

But by that time I had forgotten that I had been a lady. And for the first time in my life I was happy. I have been happy ever since.

I got to understand what America was about. That there was nothing extraordinary about me, who had come here and stayed. That was exactly what America was for, and is going to be for again someday, when the sea lanes are free again and the air open to the breath of all people. That America had gathered together undesirables and nonconformists and people who wanted to worship God in their own way; that America had opened her doors to free people who preferred taking up ax and hoe on strange soil to brandishing guns in defense of principles in which they no longer believed; that America had provided new dreams for people who were tired and restless, or who wanted to chase after newer and more colorful rainbows, as was the case with me.

All through these past thirteen years, whether I knew how I was going to pay for my dinner or not; whether I could be certain that my work was going to succeed or not; whether or not I could be sure that I would find love again, and peace of mind, I have never faltered, or disbelieved in this America of mine. I might be low at times, and discouraged; I might have a bad day and come to the conclusion that the more I knew people the better I liked flowers, and then I would stop in my tracks, take a deep breath, and then maybe whisper to myself: America. It was, and is, almost like a prayer. And I have never understood how I, of all people, had the luck to come here when the coming was good, of my own free will, not propelled out of my home as so many were after me, but propelled into a place which—in spite of the fancy homes I had had before—was the first real home I ever had.

And the peculiar thing about the whole story is that America hasn't made me rich. It hasn't showered upon me those tangible gifts which are of such great value to most people everywhere in the world. But America has taught me to work; it has taught me to take most things lightly and a very few things extremely seriously. It has taught me hope and faith and that growth and change are the only matters worth fighting for. America has made me secure. Not because I have an income or insurance, or because I can bank on anything of material value. But because I have learned that there are a few things of permanent importance, things like freedom, warmth, understanding, courage, and integrity. And a real laugh.

So there.

So there wasn't a shadow of a doubt in my mind that when the mess came to America, it meant me too. It simply meant everything that I had learned to love and cherish in these wonderful American years. It meant that if the other side won, none of us would ever have a chance again, any decent kind of chance.

...I hate war, I hate parades, I hate uniforms, I hate every kind of fight. Yet, more than all that, I hate the chance of losing America....

So I worked up my courage, wrapped it into a package, tied it securely with the few rubber bands I had left, threw it and a few books into my car, and went to this town in New England to work in munitions for The Company.

Working in munitions, as it is turning out, isn't very exciting, if you want the truth. Most of it is a filthy and grimy, much of it a very boring, job. I can't say that I love it. Very often, during the first three months, I wondered whether I would be able to take it. I wasn't too sure that this kind of life was going to work for me—me, the irrational, the spoiled and individualistic, the so-called artistic, intellectual kind of person I am. And I *hated* the grime and filth and getting up at five-fifteen in the morning and using an open latrine for a ladies' room. But neither did the men of Bataan like their grime and filth. The Chinese and Russian and Australian soldiers haven't any fun fighting, nor do the men at sea. No, there isn't any fun in this war; there isn't any fun left anywhere. This war is too damn serious, and it is too damn important to win it....

Yes, fighting and working in war plants are grim business, but somebody's got to do it, and it might as well be me. So here I go, whistling in the dark, and keeping my fingers crossed. And, anyway, it is the only way I know in which I can say, thanks, America, thanks for everything. I've had a wonderful time.

—Source: Reprinted with the permission of Simon and Schuster Adult Publishing Group from I TOOK A WAR JOB by Josephine Von Miklos. Copyright ©1943 by Josephine Von Miklos.

MARGARET HICKEY

Long a champion of women in the work force, Margaret Hickey was appointed chair of the Women's Advisory Committee at its inception. The charge of the Committee, an arm of the War Manpower Commission, was "to be concerned with the most effective use of women in the prosecution of the war effort." This constituted the first group of American women to influence major government policy during wartime. Mrs. Hickey urged local branches of national women's organizations to become involved in recruiting and training young women for this important work. The following excerpts exemplify her appeal to these groups.

The American woman has always had a job to do. First, there was the heartbreaking job of leaving the safety of the old familiar world for the risks of the new and untried.

Then there was the backbreaking job of building homes in the wilderness. It was a real wilderness. Harsh and threatening. There were no labor saving devices to make the building any easier. There was only one's own physical and moral stamina.

And even more difficult was the task of building out of these homes and by means of these homes, with their different languages and faiths and cultures, a nation—united, strong, heroic.

Certainly the greatest heritage these pioneers have passed on to us is this amazing ability, this high art, of solving difficulties, overcoming hardships, winning through. And today, in that great American tradition, we face individually and together the greatest of all tasks—the achievement of "peace on earth, good will toward men."

The first prerequisite to this achievement is victory on the battlefields. We know that "the cost will be high and the time may be long." For even though the enemy knows he's been fighting, the battle is far from won. It will require the full utilization of America's total brain and brawn. This means that no individual can escape the war. Every woman, as well as every man, must respond to the necessity of this hour....

Women in this war have proved by their works that they can rise to any occasion, that in so far as a job is concerned they can take the place of almost any man outside the actual combat forces.

By the millions, women are at their posts. They are in the armed services, in the war plants, in civilian trades and services, and on the farms.

They are working at a great variety of tasks in foundries, in aircraft factories, in shipyards. They are to be found in lumber mills handling logs; in the railroad industry—on loading platforms, in machine shops and on section gangs.

They are working as helpers in all crafts in all industries....

But the number of women at work must continue to increase....

Out of a pool of some 3 1/2 million potential workers, it would seem, on the surface, to be a relatively simple matter to obtain—say half a million. But it must be borne in mind that most of these 3 1/2 million women are inexperienced at outside work and that they also have home responsibilities. Certain resistances, therefore, must be taken into account and overcome.

In many instances, it is the husband who must be sold on the idea of permitting his wife to work. Some object because they feel it a reflection on their ability to support their wives. Others do not wish to be put to the inconvenience of readjusting to changed routine in the home.

Some inexperienced women lack confidence in themselves to do the type of work expected of them. This lack of confidence in themselves may be due partially to their feelings that many employers accept women workers only as necessary evils.

Still other women are unwilling to do many of the kinds of work for which they are needed, because of a feeling that it is too hard or too monotonous or "beneath" them.

Another resistance—perhaps the most serious—is shown to be a lack of understanding on the part of many women that the great need for their services is bona fide. Though conscious of the fact that men and women in their communities are being asked to take war jobs, some still figure, "They don't mean me...."

It is the duty of every woman to help speed the return of our American soldiers by getting into the war effort in some way. And she must get in with her hands as well as her heart. Once in, she must resolve to stick....

Today we are engaged in a terrific struggle for the survival of our democratic ideals. To this struggle we—each and every one of us—must give our best, our all if necessary, now and until Victory is ours. We cannot bring back the thousands of lives—or even one life—given to the cause. But [with] all the strength of our hands, our minds, and our hearts, we can work and hold high the torch of a living Democracy—to the end that Victory, when it comes, may be truly worth the price that we have paid.

—Source: Address of Margaret A. Hickey to the Business and Professional Women's Club, Dallas, Texas on February 2, 1944. National Council of Negro

Women Collection, Series 5, Box 38, pages 1, 3-5, 10, National Park Service—Mary McLeod Bethune Council House NHS, Washington, D.C.

2
FACTORY WORKERS

After Pearl Harbor, the conversion of peacetime industries to wartime production and the expansion of plants already producing war goods for America's allies required a large increase in the work force. Manpower alone could not fill the need. When women were called upon to join the labor force, six-and-a-half million answered the call. Good pay, love of country, or a desire to "do something" to support husbands, sons, and sweethearts who were fighting abroad motivated these women—often all three. Whatever the combination of forces that propelled them into industry, women in war production provided the needed edge to win the war.

But these women faced several obstacles in their employment: lack of training in needed skills, unfamiliarity with the often abrasive conditions of a factory environment, and a prejudice founded on the belief that the work of heavy industry properly belonged to men. Not all women could cope with these conditions. However, with endurance and determination, and a surprising adaptability, most of the new recruits took the offensive, meeting and overcoming the many challenges they faced. As they became successful in their new occupations, these "production soldiers" developed pride in their abilities and satisfaction in the knowledge that women could be effective members of a team working to win the war.

Because of the turnover of new employees, Augusta Clawson was appointed by the War Production office to join other women working in a shipyard. Her mission was to learn whether ineffective training practices were contributing to the problem. Although her factory work served only as a cover for her government assignment, she came to love and respect her craft. As time passed, Clawson discovered that her welder's job had given her a keen sense of herself as a valued member of a closely knit group, working with pride toward a worthwhile objective:

...I took a last look around, realizing again how much I love the smell of hot metal, the frying hiss of the rod, the satisfaction of laying a smooth weld, the challenge to nerves and muscles that a nasty climb involves. I've enjoyed working in the open on the deck surrounded by that blue water and those green, green hills. I have kept watch for the battleship gray of passing craft. I've checked with a knowing eye to see how the other hulls were progressing and to predict how soon ours would be ready for launching. "Ours"—I guess that's the key word. I shall miss it all frightfully because it has been *ours*: "Our Hull," "Our Gang," "Our Yard," "Our War." It's intangible, of course, like anything that really matters, and indescribably important. I've been one of a group. We've worked together, we've been afraid together, we've sweated together in the deepest tanks, and in the meanest spots in a tough job.

As a shipyard welder, Clawson also developed a fierce pride in her ability to learn and succeed in a world dominated by men, and she perhaps sensed the impact of her actions on women of the future:

I am today the proud owner of one check drawn by The Shipyard and payable to one A. H. Clawson, Badge 44651–$20.80 for three days of last week. I'll have to pay it over to Uncle Sam, but it's fun having it even go through my hands. And I shall keep the stub as a record for posterity. I must have a grandchild, even if I have to adopt one, so that I can say, "Darling, in the last war your grandmother built ships." (Probably by then my granddaughter will be an Admiral and won't be impressed at all.)

AUGUSTA CLAWSON

Many women who signed on to work in the shipyards in 1943 were leaving their jobs after only a short apprenticeship. Administrators at the U.S. Office of Education who funded training programs for war production workers worried that these women were receiving inadequate preparation. Augusta Clawson, in her role as a Special Agent for the department, was chosen to train and work undercover at a shipyard in Oregon: her official job was to assess the effectiveness of the training women were receiving. The following passages from her book, <u>Shipyard Diary of a Woman Welder</u>, *highlight what she learned about the demands of production work on women, and what she subsequently came to understand about her own strengths and capabilities.*

...I have completed six days of training, and tonight am the proud owner of two things: one—a black metal lunchbox complete with thermos; two—a firm conviction that I shall become a welder. I've had a few doubts about the latter, wondered sometimes if I could take it. No—that's exaggerated. I knew I *would* be a welder because I'd made up my mind, and I was going to do it or else.... But it was mostly a resolve, until now. Tonight I'm sure, because I'm getting such a kick out of it, and because I can see progress. Oh, I could see *some* progress before, but it wasn't fast enough to suit me. When I started, my beads looked like a very irregular mountain range. As I went on they did assume some order, and now they look more like a cable stitch in knitting. Sometimes I'd get the "feel" of welding—and then it would leave me. Again, I'd be sure I had the rhythm and I'd do about six welds fairly well—and then the next ones would be terrible! Tonight I "got the feel" and for some reason I'm confident I won't lose it again. (What a blow if I'm terrible tomorrow!)

What's more, I wish to state that *I'm getting tough*! I came in at 4:30 this afternoon bursting with energy. I showered, dressed, and went right off to town to shop. I shopped last night, but that was only because I had to. Tonight I went because I was raring' to go. I wish I had sat down and written this just before I started, because I had so much pep then. Since five o'clock I've bought pliers for handling hot plates, and the lunchbox I mentioned (so that I can join the gang at lunch). I even had time to get a bit of material so the tailor can mend a hole in my topcoat, and I left a pair of shoes to be shined.

Life is beginning to simplify. I'm quite adjusted to the new time schedule. Although I used to turn in around 1:00 A.M., now I can put out my light at 8:30 or 9:00 and go off to sleep pretty quickly. When the alarm and the telephone ring at 5:00, the *idea* feels dreadfully early, but once I'm out of bed it's no more difficult to get up than it normally is. Even my muscles are hardening, though my right wrist is still lame—especially so today; probably because I did so much weaving which is primarily wrist motion.

I find I'm acquiring a different point of view about a lot of things. It never occurs to me now to be bothered when the rain comes in on me at work. When I woke up this morning my throat was sore. Well, I thought of it off and on till I got to the yard—and haven't thought of it since. It seems to have died, perhaps through inattention. In this sort of work one just takes what comes, and that's all there is to it. I find that attitude among the other women. They do almost no kicking. They admit that one toilet is inadequate for their numbers, but they don't fuss about it.

Some of the trainees who think they aren't going fast enough will growl, "Wish *we* had Schaeffer. If we had, we'd be out of here by now. His people seem to learn faster than anyone else's." But actually each is loyal to his own instructor and there's no real resentment. It gets hotter than mustard under those heavy leathers. The tight band of the helmet makes your temples so sore that it even hurts to touch them when you're away from the Yard. The gloves make your hands sweat. The arcs give off fumes, and lots of us have burns. But no one kicks. They all take what comes in their stride....

◆ ◆ ◆

…. The sputtering and hissing and the arc's brilliant flame make everything seem fantastic and unreal. At times the whole process seems like something out of a fairy tale. Take two pieces of scrap iron, place them close together, guide the rod of metal with fire glowing from its tip, and draw it gently along the edges of these two plates and, *presto*, suddenly they are one! The terrific heat melts the metal rod and the edges of the iron plates and all the molten metal flows smoothly together. The Fairy Godmother and her magic wand have nothing on us....

The welding itself was interesting today. I started out putting a vertical bead in the angle between two plates. Then over the bead I wove metal back and forth between the two plates. The first two were rough, but the third (much to my surprise) was good. Mr. Schaeffer stood behind me and smiled (first time; he's very serious as a rule). Then he said, "That's swell." But don't think for one minute I could do the same thing again. I kept at it all morning and didn't do another as smooth. I ate lunch with about seven of the gang in a room in the school and we discussed husbands, and food, and overweight and underweight, and respective height, and relatives in the Army, and the problem of looking after young children. Two trainees hire a woman to come in and take care of their youngsters for two dollars a day. Shorty asked, "Why don't you take them to the nursery for a dollar?" One mother replied: "But the nursery opens at seven, and I have to leave at six. How am I gonna get 'em there? That nursery's no good to *any* shift. Its hours are all wrong. It ought to be open all twenty four hours."

◆ ◆ ◆

…. I crowed too soon. Today was horrible. I went in expecting to conquer the world, and was thrown by a vertical weld. I'd get it smooth about eight inches up—and then let a huge bubble roll down and spoil it. I don't understand it. Usually when you learn a thing, you retain it. But that isn't so with welding. You think you have the hang of it beautifully, and then you do welds that are inferior to day-before-yesterday's. And tonight I'm so much more tired than before. In fact, I came back from dinner, sat down in my big chair for a few minutes, and fell sound asleep sitting upright with the lights full on. I woke with a start at 7:45 to find I'd been asleep for an hour. I never did a thing like that before.

I'm certainly having new experiences. My arm aches and every muscle in my hand is yelping. Isn't it funny? Am I tired because I'm mentally discouraged? Or did I do a poor day's work because I was tired to start with, and hadn't sense enough to know it? The good old vicious circle. Jeanette Mattox had the same kind of day. I guess everyone does, for almost every day you hear someone say: "I thought I was getting it and I'm not. It's no use. I just can't learn. I'm going to quit." And next morning back each one is on the job.

◆ ◆ ◆

…. I am today the proud owner of one check drawn by The Shipyard and payable to one A. H. Clawson, Badge 44651–$20.80 for the three days of last week. I'll have to pay it over to Uncle Sam, but it's fun having it even go through my hands. And I shall keep the stub as a record for posterity. I must have a grandchild, even if I have to adopt one, so that I can say, "Darling, in the last war your grandmother built ships." (Probably by then my granddaughter will be an Admiral and won't be impressed at all.)

◆ ◆ ◆

.... I, who hate heights, climbed stair after stair after stair till I thought I must be close to the sun. I stopped on the top deck. I, who hate confined spaces, went through narrow corridors, stumbling my way over rubber-coated leads—dozens of them, scores of them, even hundreds of them. I went into a room about four feet by ten where two shipfitters, a shipfitter's helper, a chipper, and I all worked. I welded in the poop deck lying on the floor while another welder spattered sparks from the ceiling and chippers like giant woodpeckers shattered our eardrums. I, who've taken welding, and have sat at a bench welding flat and vertical plates, was told to weld braces along a baseboard below a door opening. On these a heavy steel door was braced while it was hung to a fine degree of accuracy. I welded more braces along the side, and along the top. I did overhead welding, horizontal, flat, vertical. I welded around curved hinges which were placed so close to the side wall that I had to bend my rod in a curve to get it in. I made some good welds and some frightful ones. But now a door in the poop deck of an oil tanker is hanging, four feet by six of solid steel, by *my* welds. Pretty exciting!

◆ ◆ ◆

Frank wanted me on the for'ard deck (on the fo'c'sle). There were no ladders up.... the only way to get up was to climb along the metal sides of the ship, out to the scaffolding, pull up to the top deck, and haul oneself in. It seems nothing to see the men do it; they're agile, and their muscles are in good shape. Too many of us women are soft. What one must do is step from the deck on which one is standing up to a metal brace on the side of the ship—a step as high as it seems possible to reach; then "grit" one's leg muscles and pull whatever tonnage one carries up to that step; and so on to the next and the next. My muscles have been forced to develop and harden so rapidly by the need to do this that they are like a watch spring that is wound too tight; they seem to be ready to burst through the skin. It's a queer sensation. You can certainly feel the wheels go round in this hardening-up process.

And it isn't only your muscles that must harden. It's your nerve, too. I admit quite frankly that I was scared pink when I had to climb on top deck today. It's as if you had to climb from the edge of the fifth story up to the sixth of a house whose outside walls have not been put on. Even the scaffolding around the side is not very reassuring, for there are gaps between, where you are sure you'll fall through. The men know their muscles are strong enough to pull them up if they get a firm grip on a bar above. But we women do not yet trust our strength, and some of us do not like heights. But one does what one has to. And it's surprising what one can do when it's necessary.

.... I've regained some of my self-respect. Pete came up to top deck (I think I should call it Fo'c'sle Deck) and saw me working. I had done some really good work today and he noticed it. Also Frank asked if I could work for him again tomorrow. Pete said yes. I'm delighted. I like Frank. We had quite a talk today. He had not been anxious to have women come into the work, but he speaks very highly of the work they do. He says they stick to their jobs better than the men. "You never see a woman go off and take a nap."

All things considered, this has been a red-letter day, even with that d----- climb! And the climb really adds satisfaction, since I didn't let it lick me. Everything has been fun—from this morning when we passed one of the boys from the school who yelled "Hi, girls" and we yelled back "Hi, Red!"—to seeing Missouri again. Most of all I love being up on the fo'c'sle deck. It gives you a feeling that you're lord of all you survey. I was conscious of a pride in the work we are doing, in the orderliness of the Yard, in the mechanical efficiency of the whirlies, in the accuracy of the whole job of ship-building and in the co-ordination of the various crafts. There we were—shipwrights, shipfitters, burners and welders, with helpers for each craft—all trying to beat the clock by getting that deck section laid before 3:30 p.m. We did it, too!

.... It was a crazy day. The clouds swirled over us—threatening black, and heavy gray, and a few cheerful whitish-gray ones. The rain beat down ceaselessly. Every time I inserted a rod or struck an arc I got an electric shock. The first few times I dropped the rod in spite of myself. After a bit I could make myself hang on to it. My gloves were so wet that it short-circuited. Between spasms of tacking we huddled in a wooden shed. A fire was crackling in a tall, skinny tin container, but a guard soon discovered it and took our heat away from us. My shoes were soggy and my trousers drenched. I was comparatively dry where the leathers covered me. The neck of the leather jacket got so wet that it now stands up stiffly by itself. And yet with all the discomfort I loved it.

Ways 8 is the last Ways, so there was nothing to block the view between us and the far shore of the Northwest. The rising banks were green with thick forests. Gray land barges lay at anchor outside the Yard where they had been built. A gigantic aircraft carrier passed by us so close that we could see her clearly; two pompous little tugs furnished the power. The beauty and grace of the carrier made a strange contrast with her destructive purpose, like the product of a distorted sense of humor. Her sides were camouflaged in waves of gray and white. It added to the symphony of grays made by the sky and the water, enhanced by the green of the wooded hill. The wind whipped and slashed with such strength that I had to brace myself against it as I tacked vertical clamps.

The last tack done for the time being, I started exploring. It was like looking down into a house from which the roof had blown away. I hardly recognized some of the rooms and tanks where I had worked. Open to the air they seemed little like the confined, fume-filled places I had known. With the wind whistling and the rain making a diagonal pattern against the horizon, I walked the length of the deck, hands deep in my pockets for warmth, collar close around my neck, black cap pulled down over my eyes. I realized that somehow it was thrilling. I loved the feel of the deck under my feet. I looked over each tank and compartment and felt that I owned the ship. (Wouldn't the big boss have been surprised?) Perhaps some of the blood of my sea-captain grandfather was coming out in me. If only it would last after a ship hits the rolls and the ground swells begin to do me dirt!

◆   ◆   ◆

…. I worked for an "old feller" in Port Tank 4 today. He asked whether I was "a pretty good climber." I replied, "I don't climb fancy, but I guess I can get anywhere you want me to if I go my own way." We started at the bottom of the tank, and it was as if you started from your cellar and climbed from there to the attic by means of triangular iron shelves tacked in the corner of two adjacent walls and spaced about four feet apart. It took some pulling and hauling, but I did it. Then at each shelf I'd try to fold up like a vest-pocket camera, squeeze in under a beam, and tack a piece of metal for reinforcement. I've acquired holes in the tips of two fingers of my left-hand glove. Suddenly, as I was doing a tack, braced between this triangular shelf and the scaffolding swinging behind me, a piece of molten metal slid neatly into one of the holes, lighted on my nail, and burned through to the quick. It happened quickly, and the sensation was like celluloid catching fire and going up with a whizz. One's nail is peculiarly sensitive and I didn't care for the feeling at all. I jumped, and tossed off my glove—and why I didn't plunge off the scaffolding I don't know. I guess we just hang on by blind intuition. Now I have the neatest little hole right smack in the center of my nail.

◆ ◆ ◆

…. During our morning's talk Ike commented on the fact that you could get to know people in the Yard and like them a lot, and then suddenly they left and you never heard of them again. I said yes, it seemed a shame to me to make friends there and then perhaps never see or know what happens to them afterwards. I said it with sincerity, for I'm thinking now about how soon I must leave. I shall miss these women. I've learned a lot from them. One can't despair of real democracy when one finds what I have found in this cross-section of the average American. One reads of the days of Wooden Ships and Iron Men. I salute the days of Iron Ships and Sterling Women. I'm rather proud of my sex as I've seen it building ships.

And don't talk to me about the pettiness of women. I've seen too much of the courage, endurance, and bigness of women in this Yard to listen to talk of pettiness. Here's an interesting incident showing the seriousness with which they face this work. Ella Zavoral told us that when she first did overheads she had difficulty keeping her hand steady when she had to stand on tiptoe; so she exercised her ankles constantly when she was not working by bending them inwards and outwards. "And, you know," she said triumphantly, "I can do overheads stretching on tiptoe now and I don't shake a bit."

I've always felt that there was a story behind Lil's fineness. Today she told me "There were ten of us back in Norway, but only eight grew up. Mother was widowed when I was three months old. In those days it was the ambition of most young folks to go to America as soon as they were old enough. My oldest brother left Norway before I was born. He got a job and helped to get two brothers and my oldest sister across. Then he took up a homestead and put up buildings and held it until Mother and the three little girls and one brother could arrive. I was six years old then and remember things quite clearly. We were poor, yes, but we always had plenty to eat and we were *frightfully* healthy. School was more than two miles away over the prairies. We never went in the winter, the weather was so bad." And that is the story of "Big Lil."

◆ ◆ ◆

Earning "by the sweat of one's brow" has always been just a phrase to me. Not so any more. I had a good taste of summer today, and I am convinced that it is going to take backbone for welders to stick to their jobs through the summer months. It is harder on them than on any of the other workers—their leathers are so hot and heavy, they get more of the fumes, and their hoods become instruments of torture. There were times today when I'd have to stop in the middle of a tack and push my hood back just to get a breath of air. It grows unbearably hot under the hood, my glasses fog and blur my vision, and the only thing to do is to stop.

For almost an hour I tacked on in spite of the fact that there was no blower in the room. Then I took Texas's advice and decided "no blower, no welder." I had only to suggest it, because the men for whom I was working were very nice, and they had been teasing me about the weather—my face was so conspicuously wet after only a minute or two of tacking. My work was in the poop deck where the last crew had put brackets in place *upside down.* The burner had to burn off six of them completely. For me, this meant climbing halfway up the wall and tacking them in place with horizontal, vertical, and overhead tacks. One's position is often so precarious at such an angle that it is hard to maintain a steady arc. Add to this that often I could not stand straight nor kneel. The result was that trying to hold a position halfway between would start some contrary nerve quivering so that my hand would carry out the "jiggle" and affect the weld. Yet the job confirmed my strong conviction—I have stated it before—what exhausts the woman welder is not the work, nor the heat, nor the demands upon physical strength. It is the apprehension that arises from inadequate skill and consequent lack of confidence; and this *can* be overcome by the right kind of training. I've mastered tacking now, so that no kind bothers me. I know I can do it if my machine is correctly set, and I have learned enough of the vagaries of machines to be able to set them. And so, in spite of the discomforts of climbing, heavy equipment, and heat, I enjoyed the work today because I *could do it.*

Actually the discomforts were a source of fun. I'd climb up and do a tack. I'd come down dripping, and one of the men would pick up the blower and turn it full upon me. Sometimes it would blow off my hat, and invariably it took my breath away. But it cooled me off, and I'd climb up, do another tack, and repeat the performance. My only wonder is why I don't catch cold from such extremes of heat and cold. But I don't. I believe some of us are stronger and healthier than before we did this work.

◆   ◆   ◆

…. The Boss is going to build a million-dollar nursery at Mart's Marsh. Busses that bring workers will bring the children; the cost to the parent will be 85 cents a day; and it will operate around the clock. Built like a star with blunt points, so that all the rooms get adequate sunlight, it will cover four blocks of land. Children from six months to six years old will be taken care of. She [the counselor] went on to describe other facilities being planned for older children: day camps, supervised recreation in twenty-six parks, weekly camps, 4-H Clubs, etc. Housing is also one of the services she is offering, and she took the names of any of us who were interested in this problem.

I was surprised to observe that no one took to the nursery idea at first. "I don't want my kid playing with just anybody's kids," said one woman. "My Dickie's fussy about eating. I have to watch his food," another protested. But when it was made clear that the nursery would be well staffed with doctors and nurses, that the children would receive excellent care, and that it was not "a charity thing"—their interest picked up. On the way back to the job, the group became more and more enthusiastic, and the final verdict was "Maybe that nursery is a good thing."

◆ ◆ ◆

…. The weather man had aggravated my reluctance to leave by whipping up one of those beautiful days such as only Oregon can have. The sky bright blue with billowy clouds of white and soft gray; a snappy breeze that makes you feel like conquering the world. I took a last look around, realizing again how much I love the smell of hot metal, the frying hiss of the rod, the satisfaction of laying a smooth weld, the challenge to nerves and muscles that a nasty climb involves. I've enjoyed working in the open on the deck surrounded by that blue water and those green, green hills. I have kept watch for the battleship gray of passing craft. I've checked with a knowing eye to see how the other hulls were progressing and to predict how soon ours would be ready for launching. "Ours"—I guess that's the key word. I shall miss it all frightfully because it has been *ours*: "Our Hull," "Our Gang," "Our Yard," "Our War." It's intangible, of course, like anything that really matters, and indescribably important. I've been one of a group. We've worked together, we've been afraid together; we've sweated together in the deepest tanks, and in the meanest spots in a tough job.

—Source: From Shipyard Diary of a Woman Welder by Augusta Clawson, illustrated by Boris Givotovsky, copyright 1944 by Penguin Books, Inc. Used by permission of Viking Penguin, a division of Penguin Group (USA) Inc.

CONSTANCE BOWMAN AND CLARA MARIE ALLEN

By 1943, the need for an increase in the number of war production workers was so acute the government urged teachers to work in factories for the summer vacation months. Two high school instructors, an English teacher and an art teacher, responded by training as aircraft riveters. The experiences of Constance Bowman and Clara Marie Allen, recorded in <u>Slacks and Callouses</u>, detail moments of farce and frustration but reveal as well the sense of achievement generated by their summer adventure.

....people *laughed* when we announced that the aircraft industry wanted *us* to build bombers during summer vacation. Perhaps that was why they rolled on the floor and shrieked.

You build bombers!" they howled. "An *art* teacher and an *English* teacher!"

That was the way they said it, laughing uproariously—just as if an art teacher and an English teacher *couldn't* build bombers. That was enough for us. Clara Marie said by golly, she could build bombers and I said by golly, I could too, although I wasn't quite sure what either of us could do to bombers—that would be useful. Anyhow *that* was the aircraft industry's problem. They needed help. They wanted school teachers to work during summer vacation. O.K., they had to find something school teachers like us could do.

At least we let the aircraft industry know what they were up against, for we filled out our applications for employment with perfect honesty—putting "No" or "None" after *every* question. Then, a little embarrassed at our own effrontery in thinking we could be of any use on the production line, we took our applications down to the Employment Office. We maneuvered our swooping hats into position before a tiny window which was presided over by a clerk whose name, according to the little metal standard at her elbow, appropriately was Mrs. Hires. We deposited our applications timidly in front of her.

Mrs. Hires, to our amazement, greeted our applications with expressions of joy. She didn't even look at the "No's" and the "None's." She didn't seem the least bit worried about what we could do on the production line. She just wanted to be sure that we understood ours would not be *clean* jobs. She asked twice did we understand that we would get our hands *dirty*. As soon as we had assured her that we understood—we were hired!

"Now," said the Final Induction Clerk, with a sigh as she wrote down on our envelopes the same instructions she was giving us, "you will report to Gate Two,

Plant One, at 4:30 on Wednesday afternoon. Wednesday afternoon." she repeated. "You will be unclassified helpers, final minor installations on the B-24's."

"On the *big bombers?*" we asked.

The Final Induction Clerk smiled kindly and said yes, on the *big bombers.*

"Do you have any questions?" she asked, confidently, because she knew we couldn't possibly have any. It was the final test of the efficiency of the Employment Induction.

We said no, we didn't have any questions. If we had had the strength to think of any, we wouldn't have had the strength to ask them. We felt as weak as triplicate copies of ourselves…

◆ ◆ ◆

There they were-the *big bombers!*…There was a platform of about six feet high under the wings and another about a foot high under the belly. In the back was a ladder leading up into an opening in the underside of the tail and in the front was one going up into the nose. People were all over the bombers, popping in and out of the nose, walking along the top of the fuselage, working on the high platforms under the wings, sticking their heads out the side windows, sliding flat under the belly, climbing up and down the ladder into the tail, ducking in and out from underneath, so that the bombers looked like sleeping Gullivers overrun by the people of Lilliput.

◆ ◆ ◆

If there was one night this summer that C.M. and I were ready to quit, it was our second night on the job. The second night was like the second day with a new class when they try you out, or the second day with a new teacher when she gets down to work…

Sometimes now I wonder that in my ignorance and awkwardness that second night I didn't kill someone. Once I did ingratiate myself with the administration and endear myself to my fellow workers when I dropped my drill motor down the hatch and narrowly missed the assistant foreman's head. Slightly shaken, the assistant foreman picked it up and handed it back to me. I said that I was sorry while I wondered what I would have said if it had actually landed on his head. The other people working in the ship were mightily pleased. They said that the assistant foremen was a *slave driver*, and it was a pity I had missed him. That was before I had learned that "slave driver" was practically a synonym for "foreman" in the vocabulary of the workers on the production line.

By the time that the quitting whistle blew at one o'clock, I had installed safety belt holders in all the ships on Mr. MacGregor's list. (If you're flying a B-24, you'll recognize mine because they are the crooked ones.) For every holder I had installed, I had squatted, kneeled, bent, and sat on the floor. I had gritted my teeth, clutched my motor, and pushed as hard as I could push. I had stubbed my toes, cracked my shins, and knocked my head three times on the metal sill above the safety belt holders. I had broken my fingernails, I had cut my fingers, and once I had almost bitten through my tongue, which in moments of stress I stick out and curl around my right cheek.

At one o'clock, I was tireder than I have ever been in my life-and also dirtier. My hair was tinseled with tiny shavings of metal, my hands were grimy, and my fingernails were bordered in black. My face was shiny through the smudges, my hair was tousled, and my lipstick was gone....my bright blue uniform of yesterday afternoon had a tear in the knee, a streak of grease across the blouse, and a large dusty circle on the seat of the pants where I had sat on the floor.

C.M., I was pleased to see, looked every bit as tired and dirty as I did. Together we hobbled down to the time clock while spry gray-haired women twice our age briskly passed us. Buck, the girl who delivered the electrical materials to the bomb bay where C.M. worked, stopped to tell us that one night she had clocked herself on a pedometer strapped to her ankle, and she'd found out the she had walked twelve miles during her eight hours at work that night.

"Do your feet hurt?" she asked sympathetically.

C.M. said she didn't know; she hadn't looked lately to see whether they were her feet or just the bloody ends...

At the bus stop we stood while the other women sat comfortably on the curbstone, their lunch boxes between their knees. I looked longingly at them and tentatively at C.M., but she was standing straight and composed, like a lady with standards who would never sit on the curb to wait for a bus-no matter how much her neck and arms and back and legs and knees and feet did ache. So I didn't say anything.

Finally she turned to me.

"Do you think-?" she, began, looking at the women on the curb. "Do you think that maybe-?" "Yes!" I said.

And we sat down on the curb, which felt as good as an overstuffed lounge to us at that moment.

It was two o'clock when at last we reached C.M.'s. We threw ourselves limply on the couch, C.M. with a letter from Fred, her husband.

I didn't think I was ever going to be able to get up again. I had a lumpy feeling of bruises and knotted muscles. My right hand wouldn't quite close, and the little finger was perfectly numb. The tips of all my fingers felt smooth. I asked C.M. if she thought I still had fingerprints. She looked up from her letter and said that probably I didn't so why didn't I try to crack a safe the way Jimmy Valentine used to.

◆ ◆ ◆

It was bad enough being tired all the time and dirty most of the time, but worst of all the first week was having to go to work in slacks-down Fourth Street where people who knew us acted as if they didn't, or down Third Street where people who didn't know us whistled as if they did...

It was a great shock to C.M. and me to find that being a lady depended more upon our clothes than upon ourselves. We had always gone on the theory that the only girls men tried to pick up were the ones who looked as if they could be picked up. Armed in our dignified school-teacherhood and our glasses, we were content to go unmolested with only a reassuring whistle now and then from a truck driver or a soldier in a jeep. This summer we found out that it was not our innate dignity that protected us from unwelcome attentions, but our trim suits, big hats, white gloves, and spectator pumps. Clothes, we reflected sadly, make a woman-and some clothes make the man think that he can make the woman. In our dusty blue slacks we were "Sister" and "Baby;" and even our glasses...were no protection.

Thus it was something of a problem to get home at two o'clock in the morning. Before he left, Fred had given us a short course in jiujitsu, instructed us not to speak to strangers or accept candy and rides from them, and told us to practice diligently on the living room floor the three throws he had shown us. Under strict orders from Fred, we were to alternate between Clara Marie's "attic" downtown and my house on the Point so that we could protect each other.

If we went home to the attic, we faced the problem of the servicemen who wanted to carry our lunch boxes, help us up the hill, or show us the town. One night three sailors bore down on us, swept off their caps, bowed gravely, and said in unison, "We salute you, Ladies of the Production Line, and we thank you!" We walked coolly past them, looking straight ahead...

C.M. always handled such difficult situations for us because I usually began to laugh. One night, for instance, we were climbing the hill to the attic, so dusty and tired that even our lunch boxes weighed on us like Pilgrim's burden, when two marines started to follow us, calling, "Let me carry your dinner bucket, Baby!" and "How about a little war work, Sister?" We ignored them and walked faster. They ignored our ignoring them and walked faster. We walked faster. They walked faster-until they caught up with us, one on each side. One slipped his arm through C.M.'s and the other slipped his through mine. *Now*, I thought was the time for jiujitsu. I mentally rehearsed the three throws Fred had taught us, but they all started from a position in which I was flat on my back on the living room floor. At this point C.M. came to the rescue.

She stopped so suddenly that the marine who was holding her arm was swung around in front of her.

"Sir!" she said, stamping her foot and speaking in her best classroom voice- although it did quaver a little. "Will you please stop following us *this instant*? We have been working hard all night. We're tired and we don't want to be bothered. Now go away and leave us alone, "she finished petulantly.

With this she turned on her heel, and I trailed in admiration. The two marines received her oration like the Gettysburg Address, with perfect silence. When I sneaked a look back at the next corner, they were still standing there looking after us.

◆ ◆ ◆

I...stopped at the First Aid Station for a few minutes. I explained to the nurse that I was going to tighten many fittings and that when I tightened fittings I usually cut my fingers or scraped my knuckles on the rivets of the seventh bulkhead. (There's many a Liberator in the air today with bits of my flesh clinging to its seventh bulkhead. Incidentally, I found out when I went back to school this fall that these murderous rivets had been put in at the Parts Plant by one of the students in my second period English class, and it took all my self-control to keep from flunking the boy.) I asked the nurse if she would tape all the fingers of my right hand, from the base to the tip, to protect them from the rivets. She looked at me, looked at the fingers of my right hand, and looked confused.

"Did you say that you cut your fingers?" she asked helplessly.

"No," I explained, "I just expect to cut them."

I repeated what I wanted her to do, and after a period of deliberation she decided to comply with my request. As she taped the fingers of my right hand, she said with a worried frown that she didn't know quite how to report this in her record book.

"It isn't an injury," she said, "because you haven't injured yourself yet."

"Put it down as Preventative Medicine," I suggested, as I set out for the next to the last ship.

Behind the noises of the production line I could hear a deep musical overtone like the opening notes of a great symphony played poorly on a poor French horn. On my way to the next to the last station, I stopped in front of the ship from which the sound was coming. The rubber cover on the edge of the wing was expanding and contracting in alternate tubes as the three notes blared forth.

"What makes that noise?" I asked the man standing on the platform under the wing.

"That's the de-icer," he explained, "We're testing it."

"The de-icer!" I exclaimed. "Golly, I put in the pipes for the de-icer."

The man remained unimpressed by the news, but he took time to explain the mechanics of the de-icer to me. The tubes in the rubber cover on the edge of the wing and the tail were expanded and contracted by compressed air units in the motors, he told me. The rubber cover was called a "boot" and the tubes were called "lungs." I watched proudly while the "lungs" on the edge of the wing rose and fell to the three loud notes.

"It's an awful noise, isn't it?" asked a woman who had stopped to watch with me.

"Listen, that's music," I said indignantly. "That's the de-icer system I put in."

The woman looked impressed, even if the man hadn't, and said, "My! Is it really?"

As I continued on my way down to the next to the last ship, I hummed the theme of a "de-icer symphony" I had just decided to compose some day. Mmm. Mmmmm. Mmmmm. Just those three notes that the de-icer made.

◆ ◆ ◆

We knew that a Liberator was built by many people and many hours; and whenever in a newsreel we saw the inside of a tunnel with the oxygen bottles strapped into place, the belly turret hung down in its hole, the electric wires strung neat and firm along the sides, we saw Joe throwing the bottles up into the ship and whistling "As Time Goes By;" we saw Jeff swearing ostentatiously and carefully lowering the ball turret into place; we saw Blondie and Phyllis, crisp and clean, stringing the wires and talking about their children. After a summer on the production line we looked at a Liberator the way you gaze in awe at a great tapestry when the note under it says that it took a hundred women twenty years to make it.

—Source: <u>Slacks and Calluses: Our Summer in a Bomber Factory</u> by Constance Bowman Reid, illustrated by Clara Marie Allen, published by Longmans, Green & Co., 1944; copyright ©1999 by the Smithsonian Institution. Used by permission of the publisher.

JOSEPHINE VON MIKLOS

Josephine Von Miklos began her war work as a drill press operator in a New England munitions factory; later, she became a machinist in a New York shipyard. While her motivation was primarily patriotic (see Chapter One: Leaders and Advocates), she was clearly delighted to indulge her passion for all things mechanical, as she learned the precision tool making skills that had, until then, been the preserve of men. Her sense of satisfaction was heightened when she earned praise for her new skills from a male supervisor: "You are," said the foreman, "a real machinist, Madame."

…. I got there in the first place because Miss Perry, the head of the employment office, had felt that I might have something to offer in view of the future need of mechanically minded women for the war effort. The first time I went up from New York, sometime in February, I had a long talk with her, with the head of the production department, and with a Mr. Harrington, the foreman of the department in which they thought I might start. The reason that they were at all interested in me was the fact that I knew what a lathe was, a drill press, a micrometer.

That I knew all those things had something to do with my being nuts about machines. Or, I might say, my friends in New York had always thought that I was nuts. In the course of my work as an industrial designer I had built a workshop on my roof, holding every tool dear to a mechanical heart. Instead of submitting drawings of my ideas, I had shown models in plastics or wood, and I had found that whenever a prospective client could finger a working thing, the thing was sold. Most men are like that. That I, a woman, was like that too caused raised eyebrows, a smile sometimes, often a pat on the shoulder. I could turn anything on a lathe, outside, inside, all the way round. To hold a tool or hear the buzz of a motor gave me bigger and better ideas. I don't know what made me that way, but that's the way I am.

So when the factories were advertising for skilled men, I saw my chance. And The Company saw my chance. And so they hired me…

◆   ◆   ◆

This man was standing next to me, watching me set up a somewhat intricate tool on the magnetic chuck of my migrating machine.

"You're pretty good mechanic," he said finally, and added, "for a woman."

"Why for a woman?" I asked, and wish I hadn't. I knew what was coming. I had heard it a dozen times before.

"Well," he said, and spat a hunk of chewing tobacco on the floor, "it ain't women's work."

Period.

There wasn't any use getting sore about it. There wasn't any use arguing about it. The Company had stood in The Town for a hundred and forty years and there had never been a woman in the tool-grinding room before. For a hundred and forty years men had done all the mechanical work, and who was I to revolutionize the old set up?

Day after day, as I was working among them, I would suddenly get a funny feeling in the back of my neck. I would turn around, and someone would be standing there, chewing tobacco and looking at me, my hands, and my machine; and then walking away again, not saying anything, maybe, but just looking back at me once more. There wouldn't be any expression on his face, but I knew what he was thinking. "It ain't women's work."

Well, maybe it isn't. If you divide the world in two and reserve one kind of work for the males and another kind for the females, and if you are sure that it's the best kind of world that way, and want to keep it just that way-then, of course, grinding precision tools isn't women's work.

But quite aside from the war, and this new imperative need for women to pitch in wherever they can, has it really been such a wonderful world, this great big, strong, husky male world-has it? I am not really a feminist. I am not too sure that women could do so much better if they had all the say. But I do have a very strong hunch that more real equality between the sexes might change the world just enough to put more of a permanent balance on the other side of the scale. Maybe. I don't know. We haven't really seen it yet. But we've got to try.

So somebody from the female camp had to be the first one to stick her neck out, in that particular portion of New England, and it just happened to be me. There I was, and there were 125 men watching me.

One hundred and twenty-five men watching one girl, waiting for her first scream of fright, or her first shout for help because something is too heavy or too difficult for her; that's a lot of men to live with eight hours each day, six days a week, and every third Sunday. One hundred and twenty-five fine machinists, many of whom had worked in the grinding room for more than twenty years, were a lot of fine machinists to keep up with.

◆ ◆ ◆

Charlie is an old-timer. He's been a grinder for twenty-five years and he is one of the star grinders. He could be quite a prima donna if he knew what a prima donna was. Only, it isn't in his heart...

Charlie works gently and swiftly. His sparks leave the wheel in a beautiful and regular design of stardust. Sometimes I have thought, when his head is right in front of wheel, that the sparky stardust makes a sort of halo around [his] black cap. That is, of course, a silly thing to say, because what does a halo have to do with this grimy and oily business of grinding? But maybe this is why I love grinding: the stardust gives life to steel.

Which is something that I shouldn't perhaps say to anybody. They'd surely think me screwy. Getting romantic about grinding? Phooey. It's just a job. Yes, boys, it's just a job. But I have caught you too often patting your machine, wiping your tools, singing and whistling while the sparks are flying, and I know that you feel exactly the same way about it. Maybe it *is* screwy, boys. But you can't tell me that you haven't got it deep in you, this funny passion for machines, this feeling for the high adventure through which you go when you take a piece that has no shape and make a perfect tool of it. You can't tell me that you don't love the sound of burring motors, of strength flowing endlessly through the machines. That you don't feel the thrill and the excitement in pushing your wheel just the tiniest bit more, as gently as though a mere fly had touched it, and then knowing that the job is right...

◆ ◆ ◆

...when Mr. A saw me in the grinding room for the first time he was astonished and very pleased. He watched me often as he went by. One day, as I was doing a complicated bit of measuring, he stopped and stood still until I was through, and then he smiled and looked at my work over the rim of his spectacles. Then he said:

"That is right. You do it right. Better measure three times to be sure. You are a real machinist, Madame."

I don't remember having been prouder of anything, ever.

◆ ◆ ◆

...I remembered a little scene which had happened on my first or second day among the guys...It went this way:

Another one of those guys was watching me as I was struggling over my machine.

"Hard work," he said.

"Not so bad," I answered and kept on struggling.

"Dirty too," he continued.

"I can wash," I said and kept on.

"Wait until a belt breaks on you," he said.

"It has, just a little while ago," I said, and pointed to the new belt overhead.

"You're in a tough spot," he continued, "the only girl around."

"Don't I know it!" I retorted.

"You'll burn your fingers on the wheel," he promised cheerfully, "and it hurts like hell."

I stopped and showed him the filthy, oily bandage on my hand.

"I *have* burned my fingers, and it *does* hurt like hell. But doesn't everybody around here get hurt every once in awhile?"

"Sure," he said, "but you're a woman."

"So what," I retorted a little louder, "that doesn't make me a sissy."

"Do you *like* this work?" he asked and screwed up his face.

"I *love* it," I cried and bent down again on the machine.

At last he grinned.

"You're all right," he said, and walked away.

Which seems to have been the point all along. I'm not all right for a woman, but I'm all right...

Later in the war, Von Miklos took a more challenging job in a New York shipyard.

The machine shop sits in the center of the yard, its sinews of strength. No one shop is more important than another; but in many ways there could not be another shop if there were no machine shop. The machine shop keeps the other shops going; it makes the bolts and nuts that fit armor plate into place; it makes the taps and the reamers that finish and thread the many holes through which the things run that hold a ship together. It makes the blades for the turbines which whirl and make a ship go. It makes the enormous shafts for the propellers; it repairs rusted pieces; it cuts and drills and bores, it turns and grinds and shapes the tools and parts of tools for the building and repairing of ships.

The machine shop is a great building, a city block long and half a block wide. Large trucks and overhead cranes bring and swing the pieces of ships in and out. And the noise, of course, is terrific. The men shout directions; the men shout for help; the men yell and call to each other over the din of hundreds of machines, all of them going all day, all of them going all the time, whirling and spinning and turning, inevitably and inexorably, almost like the tide which comes and goes just a few feet away, floating the ships which the machine shop serves.

It is a great machine shop, as machine shops go. You feel its strength flow into you when you enter it. You feel as though the noise and the men and the machines are giving you some of their power. Somehow I don't feel: poor little me, all lost in noise, among the men and the machines. You feel: here I am, and I am part of this, and my job is in the midst of it, and it is a good job.

And you walk upstairs into a gallery where the engine lathes are, and the diemakers' room, and the tool bins, and then, finally, the toolroom. There is glass all around you; even if the windows have not been washed for a long time, and many panes are cracked, the light comes in when dawn has faded away and daybreak has come. And there is a maze of tools and bits and machinery all around you, and, as you have felt it once before, you feel it again:

"I'll be allowed to touch all this!"

And you don't mind that many years of grease are caked over the overhead beams. You don't mind that the pulleys are creaking and whining and that the machines are covered with grit which will get deep into your skin before the first hour is half over. You don't mind that the floor is so soaked in oil that it can be washed no longer, and that the hardening oven in the far corner of the room is so badly cracked that it threatens to blow the room to pieces each time it is used.

You don't mind the smell of the fish oil that sits in a great big barrel against the wall. It has the smell of rotten sardines, and even if it makes you a little sick in the beginning, you don't mind it. The machines are old and worn out, as they are so often in a machine shop such as this; you know that you will have to be somewhat of an acrobat to use machines like these and still do the job. But you don't mind it.

You walk into a play such as this, and put your toolbox on the bench, and so you are at home and belong there. It is very important to put your toolbox in a certain place; it gives you squatter's rights and makes you an equal to the men. You know that this is where you are going to live from now on.

That's the way it is with places like machine shops and toolrooms. You feel like this or you don't. If you do, you'll be all right, in one way or another, even if not all things are sweetness and light. If you feel like this, no matter what happens, somehow you'll be all right. If you don't feel like this, you should have stayed home. It the same old story: you can't be a mechanic without the love of it in your bones.

And so I am working in the toolroom. Not as a "helper," which is the lowest form of animal in the yard, nor, or course, as a full-fledged machinist, because it "takes years" to be a machinist; but as something which is called a "second-class improver." The word implies a chance; since I have skipped the helper's and the third-class improver's stage, I might get somewhere, sometime, somehow. And even with the sound experience I have had in New England, working in the toolroom of The Shipyard is better than anything I had hoped for. You're almost somebody when you work in the toolroom. In the hierarchy of the skilled-labor world, toolmaking is tops. (And don't you think for a minute that the word hierarchy doesn't apply. It is quite as strongly developed as in other spheres of human society. Nor is it something which management alone has set up.)

I can now work with any kind of machinery, and sometimes begin a job at the beginning and go through with it to the end. (If they let me.) With my particular and peculiar kind of temperament, I sometimes get that feeling of reverence and awe over this kind of job. That feeling of service. That feeling of building and making things which make other things in a long chain of precise movements and steps. The idea than I can throw myself into the job and give it everything I have, and maybe even a little more than I knew I had. And maybe that is why I like the word "Improver."

◆   ◆   ◆

…On Mondays,…there is a Coast Guard band, playing on the stand in the yard all during the noon lunch hour. The band starts the concert with the *Star-Spangled Banner*. And as we run out from our various shops, we stop as soon as we hear that melody…the yard is full of frozen statues when that melody rings, and, rain or shine, the men take their helmets off and lift their faces up just a little, and square their shoulders, straight and hard, just like that. And on one Monday a guy next to me nudged me and whispered:

"Take your hat off, lady, you got to take off your hat."

I did. When the song stopped, and I turned to him and smiled:

"Do we women take our helmets off too?"

"Lady, "he said," you're a worker and workers take their hats off when they play this thing."

◆   ◆   ◆

...Five other girls ride with me; I pick them up at different points and we discuss in detail the various problems at hand. Our carload is a working example of American unity. We have an M.A., a B.A., two former housewives, a former librarian, and me. We come from New York, from South Carolina, from Kansas, and from Austria. Our skins are white and black. We are Catholic, Quaker, Episcopalian, Jewish, and "agnostic." One of us has a lot of money and works in the yard for purely patriotic reasons. The rest of us have no money, but we do this work because we think we must do it. Two of us think that this is just a job for the duration. The rest of us, and I am one of them, are not quite sure that we might not stick to it when the war is over. All of us, except the rich girl, are members of the union. We are working hard to make the rich woman join too. We believe that it is the thing to do. That no matter on what side of the railroad tracks we were born or have lived before, we are workers now. And that maybe some of our background and education might be helpful in building this new world in which there will be freedom for so many more people than have ever known the meaning of freedom before...

The stars are still out at this hour of the morning, and it is bitter cold now. By the time I pick my friends up, I have had my breakfast in the cafeteria, my breakfast with truck drivers and other workers who look at me understanding, although with an occasional glint of amusement. They're not quite used yet to seeing a woman in trousers having breakfast at this hour of the morning, a badge pinned to her work shirt, with a picture and a number on it. But they'll get used to it.

Driving downtown before leaving the city, I pass some of the fancy store windows around which I used to roam. Too, I pass some of the houses in which friends of mine live, and think of the parties we had together and the good, gay old times. But I don't say into their dark windows:

"How lucky you are, you can sleep."

I say:

"How lucky I am, I can go to work now. Now, while the stars are still shining, I'll be on the job when the sun comes up and by that time I will already have done an hour's work. I will see the world awaken and the waters in the docks get lavender and pink; the cranes will be moving alongside and over the ships. We'll be at work to make the ships go out into the far corners of the earth, to carry the goods of war to the men who fight for freedom. Yes, I am lucky indeed."

And I know, each day, that no matter how difficult some things will be, and how slow the work may be in coming, or how big the puzzles that are yet to be solved, I will have inched just a bit closer to the end of the war.

We hear the egg and poultry news again, as I heard it in New England. The housewives among us compare prices again. Then comes the war news, which is so much better now, and then we are at the yard. We park the car and pile out and meet the guys who are rushing in from all sides, and by now they whistle and hoot less, and we say good morning to them, and they nod to us and almost act as though they had grown used to us.

And then, maybe, I stand upstairs at the window over my bench, waiting for my next job, and I see that the aircraft carrier which has been in dock for a week is going out. She is a lovely ship. Long and slim of line, and her sides are painted with blue and gray clouds, as though some surrealistic artist had wanted to make fun of the sky and the sea.

...I hope she is sound and safe. I hope we have done right by her.

—Source: Reprinted with the permission of Simon and Schuster Adult Publishing Group from I TOOK A WAR JOB by Josephine Von Miklos. Copyright ©1943 by Josephine Von Miklos.

3

NURSES

When the Japanese struck Pearl Harbor on December 7, 1941, members of the Army Nurse Corps were already stationed at the Army Air Corps installation at nearby Hickam Field; their counterparts in the Navy were on duty at the Pearl Harbor Naval Hospital and on the hospital ship Solace in the harbor. During the course of the war, many more nurses would join the two services: more than 57,000 nurses served in the Army and more than 17,000 in the Navy during World War II. These women were sent to all theaters of the war to care for the wounded. They administered anesthesia in Africa, assisted in the removal of shrapnel in France, and helped amputate limbs in the Philippines, often toiling closer to the front lines than American women had ever worked before. Their reverence for life and deep reserve of courage and fortitude helped them not only to endure the physical hardships and danger inherent in their mission, but to provide the skilled and unflinching care the badly wounded required.

One common problem encountered by nurses close to the battlefront was the lack of adequate equipment and supplies so fundamental to the urgent care required. Often medical personnel had to respond to emergencies with resourceful improvisation. Ruth Haskell, an anesthetist on a medical team that landed in North Africa on Day-1 of an Allied invasion, later recalled the primitive conditions under which they treated the wounded. On the first night, lacking any source of electric light, they operated on those too seriously wounded to wait for daylight with only the aid of flashlights held by company corpsmen.

In France, directly behind the front lines, Captain Jean Truckey put in 16–18 hour tours of duty, trying to adequately care for the seemingly endless stream of casualties. "It is quite impossible for me to convey this scene to you, but at the height of battle the ambulances seem to start rolling in until the overflow has to lie on litters outside the receiving tent." Off duty she often slept in her steel helmet to protect herself from flak and shrapnel from heavy German artillery nearby.

The first bombing of their makeshift hospital, clearly marked with red crosses on the tents and on the ground, shocked and angered the nurses on Bataan who had depended on the "rules of war" to protect their patients. A few days later, when her ward took a direct hit, Juanita Redmond recalls she "worked wildly to get to the men who might be buried, still alive, under the mass of wreckage, tearing apart the smashed beds, to reach the wounded and the dead. These men were our patients, our responsibility; I think we were all tortured by an instinctive, irrational feeling that we had failed them."

By 1945, the nurses in the military had seen first hand the devastation of war and had exhausted themselves in their passionate devotion to their patients. "Of course, we are supposed to be accustomed to seeing handless arms, and your ears should be deaf to the groans of agony from these poor souls, *but alas the two years of combat has not hardened the heart....* Now we have finished our jobs," wrote a nurse from Italy, "we've seen the war thru. We are tired and ready to come home...."

HELEN MCKEE

In the summer of 1943, the United States Army began requiring its nurses to undergo four weeks of basic military training. Helen McKee, a nurse anesthetist, was one of the first members of the Army Nurse Corps to be tested on an obstacle course that used live ammunition to simulate battle conditions. Four months later, in Naples, Italy with the 300th General Hospital group, she was also among the first to witness the astonishing power of a new British drug, penicillin. With its use, "grossly infected wounds" caused by shrapnel, flak, and bullets were cleaned up in only three to five days and the necessary grafting of skin over the affected areas could begin.

Camp Forest, Tennessee
May 6, 1943

Dear Mother and Dad:

Who dreams up all these little fun and games activities we have engaged in lately? The latest was a ten mile forced march with all manner of diversions en route....

But the real fun comes in marching with the gas mask on. You can get an adequate amount of air, but none to spare, especially when you are force marching. That was only part of the entertainment provided us. Someone came up with the idea of giving the air corps a little practice in bombing, and us a little practice in ducking.... You run for cover, throw your gas mask back and fall, your elbows catch your body, and your face remains off the ground. This is to prevent concussion from exploding bombs.... When we finally reached our destination, Cumberland Springs, we climbed down a hill, took off our shoes and sox and waded in the cool spring water. My, but it felt good. We then had our rations which consisted of two sandwiches, coke or coffee and cake. Hardly an adequate meal for a hard working soldier.

Mother and Dad, I think you are to be congratulated on producing such a sturdy offspring...

Deepest love to all,

Helen

Camp Forest, Tennessee
July 18, 1943

Dearest Ones:

After doing a ten mile forced march with full field pack some time ago, we thought we had triumphantly met the Army's ultimate challenge. But the final test of our physical stamina was to be encountered on the infiltration course.... It was about the most thrilling, completely rugged adventure of my life.

First, there was the matter of suitable attire. I sought out the smallest soldier in the 300th, and borrowed his fatigues. At that my arms and legs were lost, so I borrowed a pair of leggings to hold up the pants legs. I soon mastered the trick of wrapping them around my legs. Next came the assembling of our field equipment: canteen, gas mask, pistol belt and steel helmet. What a motley assortment we were as we climbed into trucks to be taken to the infiltration course, which was an area one hundred yards in length with a trench at both ends. The trenches were four feet deep and half filled with water and mud. At one end, overlooking the course, were two towers from which machine gun fire and explosions were directed, and from which blared forth directions and warnings....

We were allowed a few minutes of "at rest" following our unloading from the trucks. This enabled us to adjust to the assault on our ears of the rat-a-tat-tat of the machine gun fire and the boom of the dynamite explosions. Then an infantry officer gave the orders, "Fall in." We fell in. "Right Dress." We dressed right. "Front." We fronted. "At ease." We were at ease, and he went over the plan and the procedures of the course. He demonstrated the best infantryman crawl, and then explained that machine gun bullets would be aimed two feet above our heads. This bit of information seemed to make the subsequent instructions superfluous; but nevertheless, he continued, "Keep your heads down, your hands, arms and feet down." Then he thundered, "And keep your fannies down." We adjusted our helmets, made sure our pistol belts, canteens, etc. were correctly positioned. "Attention," came the next command, "left face; forward march; route step; halt." We were standing at the edge of the starting trench. Here he instructed us to crawl down into the ditch. It was about waist deep in slush. As we parted he warned us to take our time, adding that the infantryman's average time for the course was twelve minutes, but that he expected no better than thirty minutes from us. We were then on our own.

The signal to start firing followed, and my troubles began. As instructed I braced my body on the front of the trench, but my legs were too short to reach it, and that is the only way you can go over and still hug the ground as you emerge. So I waded down to a point in the trench which appeared a little narrower, and tried once more. This time I succeeded. Once out of the trench I found that the mud was no longer my enemy, for it was easier to slide in the slush and slither along the ground than to pull one's body over dry terrain.

In the meantime the rat-a-tat-tat became a part of you and you knew the boom would follow shortly, and you sensed that all was well and you were on your way. I think each of us was filled with a grim determination to finish and in good time. After about fifty years of crawling on my tummy, I found the first strand of barbed wire which was stretched across the course at the half-way point. I lay still a few seconds rehearsing the procedure; then deliberately rolled over on the side opposite my canteen, etc., onto my back, reached behind me, drew the first strand of wire forward, moved my body through, letting the strand go as I reached for the next strand. Just at that moment a blast went off nearby and I was caught facing upward. A shower of mud came down on my face. Since I was in barbed wire entanglement there was no choice except to let go and continue. I clearly remember counting nine such strands of wire that had to be negotiated.

With that obstacle behind me I again rolled over and set out for the remaining fifty yards, slithering through the mud. We were beginning to feel muscle strain and becoming aware of scratches and bruises around elbows, knees and hips. I heard a booming voice from the tower, "Sergeant, move to the right. You are headed toward a mine." The message came through a second time before I realized I was the endangered species, for the attire I had borrowed for this occasion bore a sergeant's stripes.

At last my outstretched hand caught the bank of the trench. I maneuvered around to a side position and rolled over the bank into the trench. The muddy water felt almost refreshing after expending so much energy in the intense mid-afternoon heat.

Ninety percent of the girls, including myself, had completed the course in fifteen minutes, and we had been allowed thirty. We sat there neck deep in water until the "all clear" signal was given.

The gun fire had ceased and now new sounds greeted our ears. An army band had been trucked in while we were so intently involved in covering the course, and as we emerged from trench, covered with mud, the band struck up with "O, You Beautiful Doll."...

My deepest love to all of you,

Helen

[Naples, Italy]
November 19, 1943

Dearest Mom and Dad,

…What do you think? I gave the first anesthetic given in the 300th General Hospital on foreign soil, here in Italy. We fought hard to save this dreadfully wounded lad, even to flying in from England a supply of a new drug, which is not yet available in the U.S. It is called Penicillium. Sorry to say, however, I don't believe he is going to make it. Honestly, it tears your heart out by the roots, but we don't talk about that. The morale must be kept high. No one dares to let down. Of course, we have endless numbers of shrapnel wounds, flak wounds, bullet wounds, and every sort of wound imaginable, but we also have the same old things, hernias, tonsils and the regular old line from Camp Forest, but most of it is war casualties. Working over here is completely different from stateside. We have learned that each little scrap must be utilized. We have learned to work without materials we considered absolutely necessary. For instance, we have no CO_2 for our machines, no soda-lime, no pins, either straight or safety pins, and paper is so scarce…

Love from the depths of my heart,

Helen

[Naples,] Italy
February 8, 1944

Dear Folks,

…Last Sunday I had one of "those" anesthetics—He had a piece of flak in his lung, and Col. Pistine chose Sunday morning to do it. As a matter of fact the anesthetic began at 0845 hours and ended at 1145 hours. It was—as all Lung decortications we do, Pentothal induction, Gas Oxygen and Ether Anesthetic, endotracheal, and it went swell. Honestly, I say as I tap on wood,—I've not had a gummed up anesthetic in the past six months…. These cases are very difficult, naturally, since the good lung is on the down-side—the bad lung on the up-side—You can see how position in this case would tend to create a difficulty in respiration. There are so many complications that can arise out of this type of operation—really is quite a risk, and I usually feel a little unstrung just before I start one, but once I get a gas mask in my hand there is something just short of a miracle—I get just as calm and matter of fact at that point and from there on I never have a qualm over my anesthetic....

I love all of you very much,

Helen

[Naples,] Italy
March 7, 1944

Darlings:

...Within the past three days our department has slackened its work to some degree. We are still definitely earning our room and board plus the salt in our bread which is obviously lacking at the present, and will be until a ship comes thru.... We do, thank goodness, still have salt for the plaster casts, and after all that is the most urgent use we have for salt here. We are still doing a land-office job on orthopedics and the Penicillium ward is going strong. The results are marvelous—most unlimited results. Can you imagine these grossly infected wounds, covering a large area, mostly with bone fragments protruding up into the wounds. We used Penicillium on some of these cases for a period of three days and found the wounds practically clean and healthy at the end of the third day period. As soon as the bone fragments are covered over, we do skin grafts. It looks so crazy to see these great depressed areas. This is so new we have not been able to tabulate our case outcome, but we are watching with eagle eyes. Day before yesterday I spent my entire day with Penicillium patients. So far as we know the drug is not obtainable for civilians either in the States or in England. Of course you know that Penicillium is of English origin. I am sure you have read of Prof. Fleming's discovery, quite by accident [British bacteriologist Alexander Fleming developed the antibiotic penicillin]. One thing on which a great deal of stress is laid is the fact that Penicilium without proper debridement of wounds just does not work. To sum the matter amounts to this: early and sufficient debridement, Penicillium 3 to 5 days—skin graft!...

Mom, by the way I did want to tell you, while on the subject of skin grafts, these grafts are secured either by a plain everyday little basting stitch or a tailor's stitch off a spool of #40 white cotton, just the same cotton you have there on the machine in the brown wicker basket. You still have it, I hope....

Love,

Helen

Same Place [Naples, Italy]
June 25, 1944

My Dear Ones,

…. Both during the Anzio beachhead landing, and Cassino drive, our patients came to us with only first aid care. We debrided their wounds, did the amputations, took slugs out of the livers and removed their shell fragments from all vital organs. We cleaned them up—killed the maggots in their wounds and *put them to bed between clean sheets.* Four days later they came back to surgery and we did our Gen. Hospital job. Secondary closure, bone plating, grafting both bone and *much, much* skin. We operated on their spines removing foreign bodies and fracture fragments (Laminectomy). We decompressed head fractures and dug foreign bodies from the lungs, diaphragm, every type of surgery imaginable.

Let me tell you about one evening last week when I was on call and was sent for. I had a very acutely ill patient on the table.—Terribly irregular pulse and his breath was so labored. I put him to sleep with Pentothal and in short order, Major Burford had the man's heart in his hands and I do mean literally—He opened the outer lining of the heart (pericardium) removed a shell fragment the size of the last phalanx of my little finger, picked out numerous scraps of woolen O.D. [olive drab] shirt and drained the abscess. The patient's pulse was regular on leaving the table and his blood pressure had picked up wonderfully—That, my dear, was pericardiotomy. One of the few I've ever seen in my life….

Love,

Helen

May 25 [1945]

…. This war lasted just a bit too long for [one] boy—just another few days and he would have had his eyes and his left arm. I shan't forget, very soon, the sudden nausea that overtook me when I realized it was a matter of enucleating both eyes instead of one. Of course, we are supposed to be accustomed to seeing handless arms, and your ears should be deaf to the groans of agony from these poor souls, *but alas the two years of combat has not hardened the heart,* nor hardened the soul but, praise God, their days of "wounds due to enemy action" have ceased. You know at times I still feel sort of numb to anything except the fact that casualties have ceased to be. I don't think anyone felt closer, or shared the pain of these boys than we, the A.N.C. Now we have finished our jobs, we've seen the war thru. We are tired and ready to come home.

Helen

—Source: "Letters, May 6, July 18, November 19, 1943; February 8, March 7, June 25, 1944; May 25, 1945" by Helen McKee from <u>We're in This War, Too: Letters from American Women in Uniform</u>, edited by Judy Barrett Litoff and David C. Smith, copyright ¬ 1994 by Judy Barrett Litoff and David C. Smith. Used by permission of Oxford University Press, Inc.

MARTA GORICK

Former school nurse, Marta Gorick, joined the Army Nurse Corps as a lieutenant in August, 1942. In January of 1943, the troopship on which her group of nurses was being transported to North Africa was torpedoed by the Germans. Gorick managed to keep her perspective and her American sense of humor throughout the ordeal: after being rescued from a lifeboat by the crew of a British destroyer, she wrote about her misadventure to a friend at home, commenting on the loss of clothing she had expected to last for the duration of the war: "My five lovely girdles! Maybe some shark is wearing them now…"

Somewhere in Africa, 1943

Dear Mag,

…. I suppose by now you know that we were torpedoed…

It was a beautiful moonlight night—too much so—when we were torpedoed. It was in the wee hours of the A.M. and I had just gotten sound asleep, after promenading the deck, when I heard this distinct thud and there was no doubt in my mind as to what had happened. The engines stopped and there was a dead silence. I jumped out of my bunk and yelled to the other two nurses to hurry up and dress, as we had been hit. The lights were out, so we hurriedly dressed by flashlight. I put on my slacks and long blue coat, grabbed my blue skirt and jacket, and tied my blue muffler over my head. I then put on my "Mae West" (lifebelt to you), grabbed my pocket-book, and as I was leaving the cabin (as usual, thinking of my stomach), I picked up a few oranges, which were on the table.

We went on deck, where we were lowered down in lifeboats and as this was being done, a gush of oil sprayed up, as we were being lowered from the side that the boat had been hit. I did not have a place to sit as the lifeboat was filled to capacity. So I stood in the lifeboat. My legs were wet to my knees as there was quite a bit of water in the lifeboat. We had also brought our helmets with us, so we all bailed like the dickens, besides rowing the boat, as the motor went dead.

My one knee shook for about an hour after the torpedoing. The lifeboat was rocking, and, you know, I never thought of getting seasick in a lifeboat but all of a sudden one of the English Sisters across from me started and before I realized it, I was keeping her company. Quite a few, in fact most of the people eventually did the same, so that our helmets were very busy.

After two or three hours the people were shifted around so that I finally got a seat. Quite a few men were picked up from rafts and some of the boats had some very sick and injured people on them. It seemed like a dream. However, all of the women acted like bricks. I finally nodded myself to sleep, as a destroyer came along and through a loud-speaker announced that we would be picked up later in the A.M. We were all soaked and cold but it could have been a lot worse.

We were in the lifeboat about seven and one-half hours and then we were picked up by a destroyer. I put on my rouge, lipstick, and powder before being picked up, thinking I might look at least a little bit glamorous, although worn-looking. The Britishers on the destroyer served us hot tea and sandwiches and quite a few of the sailors lent their clothes to the people who were soaked. I sat out in the sun and let the sun dry me up. You would laugh to see these tough sailors promenading through, carrying women's unmentionables to dry.

When we finally landed, I only wished I had had a movie camera. Talk about costumes and outfits! One very dignified matron of the British Sisters (nurses) came strutting down the gang-plank in her stockinged feet, and long pajamas, but with her head up and chest out. You also would have laughed at the clothes they first gave us. The American soldiers and officers gave us cigarettes, candy, socks, shirts, trousers and even B.V.D.s. Then the next day they went out shopping to buy some ladies' underwear.

I was one of the fortunate few to save my pocketbook, which contained all my money, fountain pen, rosary, my Army papers, vanity case and a few other toilet articles. For several days that vanity case and comb were used by most of the girls in my outfit so that it was soon depleted.

And to think I ran myself ragged shopping for stuff and things to take with me! Oh well, they can be replaced but there's only one of me, huh? However, if I ever get my hands on the Jerry who shot that torpedo, I'd choke him. My five lovely girdles! Maybe some shark is wearing them now....

You should have seen us in men's B.V.D.s. Really we cut quite a figure. I had to laugh because our chief nurse told us to be sure and be in full uniform and look real nice when we landed in Africa.... To think yours truly landed with just what she had on her back, plus a pocketbook....

...I'm thankful yours truly is here. As I've said many a time and I still say, "God has been good to me," or else only the good die young.

Marta

—Source: "Letter, Somewhere in Africa, 1943," by Marta Gorick in <u>With Love, Jane: Letters from American Women on the War Fronts</u>, ed. Alma Lutz, The

John Day Company, 1945, in the Archives of John Day Company, Department of Rare Books and Special Collections, Princeton University Library.

RUTH HASKELL

After volunteering to leave her comfortable position at an Army hospital in Tennessee and her young son, Carl, with his grandparents to serve overseas, 2nd Lt. Ruth G. Haskell was assigned to the 48th Surgical Hospital Unit. On the eighth of November, 1942, this team of surgeons and nurses landed in Algeria within hours of the first military contingent of Operation TORCH, an Allied offensive in North Africa. Their arrival in this "hot" territory was greeted by snipers who continued to harass the three nurses and four surgeons who later that night made their perilous way to a temporary evacuation hospital. There they discovered "the unmistakable odor of filth and dirt, mixed with the odor of old blood and stale ether," as they viewed "Rows upon rows of American boys…on litters all over the floor," waiting for medical aid and relief from pain. In the account of her experiences, <u>Helmets and Lipstick</u>, Haskell comments, "There has never been a time that I have been so proud to be a nurse, to be able to help."

Here we were, huddled down on the tile floor of a deserted beach house, while outside was the steady sound of artillery fire and the sky bright as day, at times, with the light from the bursting mortar shells. Our only piece of furniture was a rectangular table which stood in the center of the room. All the windows in the place had either been shot out or broken from concussion, and it was rapidly becoming cold, very cold. Our clothing was still damp from the ducking we had received in the Mediterranean, and we had no cover….

Gradually we became quiet, but we did not go to sleep. It grew colder as the floor grew harder—by the minute! Edna had just finished wiggling around trying to get comfortable, when the back door flew open and the Colonel's voice boomed out in the darkness.

"Atkins, Kelly, and Haskell. Report to headquarters immediately. Wear all your equipment, and bring your gas masks!"

◆ ◆ ◆

…one of the enlisted men was waiting…to take us to headquarters about a hundred yards away in another ancient cottage.

…we found the Chief Nurse, our Colonel and the Corps Surgeon, who had come in from a small village four miles away. "All Hell's to pay up the line," said the Colonel, "and we have to have help. The boys at the battalion aid station can't handle the casualties, they're coming so fast."

Just as he finished talking, the door burst open again and in came two of our surgeons.

Captain Borgemyer said, "What's it all about, what's up?"

Captain Markham just beamed his genial smile and waited for someone to volunteer the information as to why he had been called out of his nice comfortable foxhole.

The Chief Nurse gave each of the three of us a box of morphine surrettes and a hypo syringe.

"Goodness knows what you will find up there," she said. "But do as good a job as you can, and at least these will help those God-blessed boys if the pain gets too bad."

The two surgeons had a supply of sedatives and narcotics, and at last we started off—an eerie little procession of three girls and four men. The jeep, we understood, had been left some distance back from where we were bivouacked.

It was very difficult to walk in the loose and sliding sand, especially as we seemed to be walking uphill. You couldn't see your hand before you, until all of a sudden the sky would be bright for just a second as another shell reached its mark. The backs of my legs were beginning to ache, and I began to understand why the Colonel had insisted on our drilling and having road marches back in England.

Just then there was a queer whistling sound, and the enlisted man on ahead said quickly, "Down!"

Before I had a chance to drop, he had pushed me by the shoulder and down I went.

"What was that?" I asked.

"Damned sniper somewhere taking a pot shot at us. The dirty bastard!"

Surely such doings were not to be taken lightly, and I'll confess that when I got back onto my feet and we started on again, I did so with a very queer feeling around my heartstrings.

Kelly and Atkins were both little girls, and I was a great big husky brute. I wondered how they were standing it, because I knew that I, for one, was getting plenty tired. In fact I had just about decided I would drop from exhaustion, when a dark object loomed up in front of us that turned out to be the jeep.

Now, I had driven one of the things in the States and been joy-riding in them in England. But I certainly felt more apprehension about swinging my slack-covered leg up over the side of this one than any other one I had ever laid eyes on.

I got in first, and then Captain Borgemyer tossed first Edna in behind me and then Kelly. The rest of the party got in, and we started off, a soldier with a tommy gun on each front fender. Somehow I didn't know whether to feel better or worse about their being there. I must confess my emotions were rather mixed at this point. Then I discovered that the man riding behind us also held a tommy gun protectingly in the corner of his arm. Shades of my Irish ancestors!

We drove maddeningly along for a few hundred yards, when suddenly right out of nowhere popped a sentry. He shouted the password and the Colonel the countersign, which, of all things, was the gag line of one of our most popular comic strips! (I thought: Of all things, at a time like this to play games!) This happened at regular intervals along the four-mile route, and every time it did, we almost choked to keep from laughing. So it wasn't such a bad idea.

Finally we began to enter what looked to be a town. The Colonel said, "This is Arzeu. The place I am taking you to is right in the heart of this town. Be on the alert, for snipers have been taking shots at us all evening."

He had hardly stopped speaking before: *bang, bang, bang, bang*. Four shots whistled by our heads, close enough for us to feel the breeze from them. My heart was going like a triphammer, and the Colonel said, "See what I mean?"

We saw all right, and as one, the whole group sank down lower in the seat. We drove slowly along streets that were narrow and furtive, lined with palm trees that swayed in the breeze. Occasionally one could hear the echo of a shot from the other side of town and then a series of them, too near for comfort. Soon we turned into a short street, and I don't think the band on an M.P.'s arm ever looked so good to me as did the one a certain boy was wearing who stood guard outside what appeared to be a high fence enclosing some sort of compound. He shouted that silly little old password, a voice from inside the jeep gave the countersign, and the gate was opened just wide enough for us to walk through.

I was so stiff and cramped from being crowded in the jeep that I could hardly move. And so were the others. But when a sudden shot kicked up the dirt in front of us we moved, and fast!

It was discovered a little later that our friend who had greeted us so rudely was perched on a housetop across the street. Nice playful little fellow, I thought grimly.

"What sort of a place is this?" I now asked of no one in particular. From what I could see in the darkness, it appeared to be a rather square building about three stories high. A guard volunteered the information that it had been used by an old French midwife for an obstetrical home before the war.

As we reached the door, the guard shouted for them to extinguish their flashlights, that someone was coming in. We waited a second, then a blanket was pulled back—it had been rigged outside the door—and we stepped into the room.

The first thing that struck you were the odors. The unmistakable odor of filth and dirt, mixed with the odor of old blood and stale ether. There was a suppressed groan here and another there, and then a voice over in the corner: "May I have a drink of water? I've had nothing since three o'clock this morning." It was now nine-thirty, and the Lord only knew what the lad had been through in those hours!

One of the boys flashed on his light, and I shall never forget the sight that spread out before my eyes in that room. Rows upon rows of American boys lay on litters all over the floor. Just barely enough room to step over them to get around. There were pools of blood beside some of them, where dressings had not been changed sine the first shock dressing was applied in the field. I don't know how the other girls felt, but I experienced at once a violent anger—bitter, surging anger—against a people that, out of greed and power and lust, would cause such things to happen to young manhood.

We found that we were to help in surgery with the boys who were most seriously wounded. The captain in charge of the group had one of the enlisted men take each of us through the building in an effort to weed these out and have them brought to the second floor, where a surgery of sorts had been set up. As we walked along, and the beam from the flashlight played over the faces of these boys, it was evident they were all in intense pain. But not a word of complaint was being uttered. Every mother with a son in this war, I thought grimly, could be proud of the sort of man he turns out to be under fire!

We climbed the moldy stairs to the second floor. It was very cold up there, as most of the windows had been blown out, and unlike the first floor all the openings were not covered with blankets. Rats were nosing about at will, but we hardly noticed them. As I straddled a litter to continue across the hall, a boy looked up at me and asked, "Please, is there any water anywhere? I'm terribly thirsty."

Now we had been told that the quart of water we had in our canteen was all we would get until a water point could be established. But what nurse could refuse such a request? Without a moment's hesitation, I bent down and, supporting the boy's head in my hand, helped him to drink from my canteen. As he dropped back onto the liter, gasping a little from pain, I asked, "Is that better, sonny? Where do you hurt?"

There was a moment's silence and then: "My God! A woman, an *American* woman! Where in heaven's name did you come from?" He was almost sobbing as he finished.

There has never been a time in my life that I have been so proud to be a nurse, to be able to help.

"Yes, sonny," I said. "An American woman, a nurse. And there are sixty of us from home over here to take care of you...."

◆ ◆ ◆

...we all proceeded into the room we were to use for surgery. That room was something to behold. An improvised operating table in the center under a drop light with about a twenty-watt bulb in it (which, incidentally,, burned out within the next few minutes), a small handbasin and spigot. The water just dribbled from the spout, for the regular supply had been cut off by the French before we took over the town. A huge packing case for the anesthetist to use for a stool, one table, a small sterilizer that burned alcohol, a scalpel, a mere handful of clamps, and a pair of surgical scissors completed our equipment. It was positively heartbreaking when one thought of all the excellent equipment standing on board ship in the harbor.

The corpsmen found some flashlights, and we got ready to start the biggest night's work in our lives. Luckily the battalion aid field chest contained a fair quantity of alcohol and sutures, and plenty of ether and sulfa drugs. The doctors had rolled up their sleeves and were washing their hands in a basin of alcohol.

Gone were the elaborate gowns, masks, drapes, and towels that all nurses associate with surgery. The first boy brought in had a huge bayonet slash on the inner side of his left upper arm. When one flexed his elbow, the brachial muscle popped in and out of the slash as though it were supposed to do so. We cut the sleeve out of his shirt on that side and, so far as the patient was concerned, this constituted the preparation....

...A nod to Kelly and she passed Captain Borgemyer the pitifully few instruments we had to work with. Kelly had her G.I. flashlight fastened to the band of her slacks, and that was all the light she had to work with in doing her job of trying to keep sterility where the instruments were concerned. The corpsmen were holding flashlights with the beam trained on the incision, and I couldn't help remembering how many times surgeons I had worked with in hospitals at home had thrown well-regulated fits when the lighting system wasn't just to their liking.

Soon one of the dentists relieved me at the post of anesthetizing, as I found that my rather small hands became tired very quickly holding the jaws of those men. I joined Kelly and helped get together more sutures and drains, for supplies were dwindling fast.

Boy after boy was sent in, operated on, then sent back to bed on a litter on the floor. I relieved the dentist at intervals, and it was during one of these periods that I nearly lost my life. Edna, who had been circulating among the wounded on the floor below, giving hypodermics here and there to make the going easier, had just entered the operating room to ask a question of the doctor. By opening the door she had innocently created a draft, causing the blankets over the window to blow ever so slightly.

Bang!

Instinctively I ducked as a bullet whistled past me and ricocheted off the wall behind my back. Believe me or not, I could feel a breeze as the wretched thing missed my head by inches!

There was a short interval of silence, broken by the oaths that sprang from every mouth in the room. Apparently a sniper in a tree outside the window had shot at the glimpse of light when the blanket moved.

I have never seen a more incensed group of men than those in that room at the time. This happened not once but again and again through the night. Finally there was the sound of two shots outside the building, a dull thud as of a body falling to earth, and a cry. Then we weren't troubled any more. I wouldn't have believed it possible to get so much positive exultation as I did over the death of that sniper.

—Source: <u>Helmets and Lipstick</u> by Ruth G. Haskell, published by G.P. Putman's Sons, 1944.

JEAN TRUCKEY

Head nurse Captain Jean Truckey served with the 67th Evacuation Hospital group as it followed closely the advance of American troops liberating the territories of France after D-Day. Near enough to the front lines to be kept awake at night by artillery fire, she and her nurses treated wave after wave of battle casualties who were brought to them with the most horrific wounds. Despite the mind numbing fatigue of 16 and 18 hour days, Truckey was able to observe and subsequently describe in graphic detail the grim details and incongruities of war.

At the Front in France
June 18, 1944

Dear Ruth:

We were lucky to reach here safe and sound—dirty and tired. We've been working with another evacuation unit but move out in the morning, farther up, to set up our own hospital and be ready for patients by noon.

At the moment I'm sitting among a bunch of bed-rolls and duffle bags, out in the field, just above the hospital. I'm quite tired—had a shower this afternoon, which was wonderful. The first time I've had my clothes off in three days. Took off my shoes yesterday and my leggings, to wiggle my toes, for the first time in 36 hours.

The artillery fire is getting louder with night coming. At 11 p.m., the Jerry bombers come over and then the fun starts. I never could imagine such noise in my life. Like the Fourth of July multiplied a million times. The ground trembles. We lie there and wonder, and if it's too close, we stick our steel helmets over our heads.

Last night we slept on the ground, but in tents. Tonight we are lucky to have cots and tomorrow night we'll be in our own area, in our own tents, with cots to sleep on and our sleeping bags. Wonderful! I have to stop every few minutes to look up at our wonderful protective planes flying all over.

Please pass this letter among you, for from now on I just shan't have the time to write much. We're so tired when we're off duty we just fall down and sleep.

As for our soldier boys—words fail me. None of you back home can ever understand. You would never, never utter a word of complaint over anything, nor gripe about anything in the world, if you walked into our hospital. These boys never complain. They are quiet and patient. I was by one as he died this afternoon—just after an operation. His trachea had been completely severed. No need to go into details, for you just can't grasp it. At least we are happy to be doing all in our power to help.

There are eight brain operations scheduled for this evening so I'm going to call this quits. There are also about six Frenchwomen as patients here. They were caught between the lines of fire and were badly injured.

They all treat the nurses with consideration—the officers and soldiers both. And the fighting men are delighted to see us.

June 20

Just a hasty note while off duty for an hour. Our hospital has been functioning in another area since yesterday morning. We travel by truck from one site to the next and yesterday was an eye-opener. Drove right through places where the battles had raged a couple of days previously.

Here are a few hasty impressions, gleaned in transit: Shell-pocked road signs reading, "Roads Cleared of Mines to the Hedge." Villages completely destroyed. Newly-made graves. German and American helmets and equipment strewn everywhere. Colored parachutes dangling from trees. Gliders smashed to kindling wood and many partly submerged in water. Gardens full of artichokes. Old orchards full of foxholes. Dead cattle and horses. Red and yellow roses climbing ancient stone walls. A huge stone crucifix with Christ hanging with bowed head. Fields full of red poppies. Old French men and women with wooden shoes. Bewildered women and children looking through ruined homes. Over-turned tanks and trucks. Tired, dirty, unshaven soldiers whose faces broke into smiles at the sight of American nurses. The heavy roar of gunfire like a big, constant thunderstorm—and then our hospital completely identified with Red Crosses. Twelve and 16-hour duty tours and finally bed at about 11 p.m. The first time out of my fatigues in four days. It was wonderful to slip into woolen pajamas and into my bedroll.

June 26

.... [One] evening I went to as many cots as I could to remove the men's big, heavy, dirty shoes. It sounds so trivial, but many had not had their shoes off in 18 days and they were so grateful just to wiggle their toes. Their shoelaces and leggings were just about imbedded in their shoes. They slept in ditches and foxholes.

It is quite impossible for me to convey this scene to you, but at the height of battle the ambulances seem to start rolling in until the overflow has to lie on litters outside the receiving tent. It's something Hollywood hasn't coined words for....

These men are magnificent. Quiet and uncomplaining, even when almost dead. One man had 15 fractures and 19 big wounds. Another had his buttocks blown off. Another had the lower half of his face blown off. A specialist worked on him for three hours. Even his tongue was shot off. But the poor boy lived only a day. We also have some gas gangrene cases and some are pitiful. One with both arms amputated; another, his legs amputated. But maybe I ought not to write you these sordid details.

My nurses are wonderful girls. We work from 16 to 18 hours a day. The men are so happy to see American women. One young boy told me the other night I was the first one to tuck him in since he left the States. Just like little boys. My first thought when one has passed away is his folks back home. We surely do all we can for them....

My biggest complaint is that I can't sleep well at night, even though I'm very tired, because of the heavy gunfire. It is so close that we often sleep with our steel helmets on. If some flak or shrapnel came through the tent, seems to me my head would be somewhat protected....

Jean

—Source: "Letters At the Front in France, June 18, 20, 26, 1944," by Captain Jean Truckey in With Love, Jane: Letters from American Women on the War Fronts, ed. Alma Lutz, The John Day Company, 1945 in the Archives of John Day Company, Department of Rare Books and Special Collections, Princeton University Library.

JUNE WANDREY

After graduating from nursing school in Minnesota in December of 1941, June Wandrey immediately joined the Army Nurse Corps. She subsequently served in field and evacuation hospitals in North Africa, Sicily, Italy, France and Germany. Because of her work near the combat zone in several campaigns, she received seven World War II battle stars. She served her final overseas assignment as an Army nurse in Allach, Germany, in 1945, caring for the "corpse-like patients" who had been liberated from the concentration camp at Dachau. The difficulty of working at this post is clearly apparent in a letter written to her family: "It's a corner of hell. Too shocked and tired to write anymore. Love, June."

6-4-45 Allach, Germany

Dearest family,

I'm on night duty with a hundred corpse-like patients, wrecks of humanity…macerated skin drawn over their bones, eyes sunken in wide sockets, hair shaved off. Mostly Jewish, these tortured souls hardly resemble humans. Their bodies are riddled with diseases. Many have tuberculosis, typhus, enterocolitis (constant diarrhea) and huge bed sores.

Many cough all night long, as their lungs are in such terrible condition. They break out in great beads of perspiration. Then there is the roomful of those that are incontinent and irrational. It sounds like the construction crew for the tower of Babel…Poles, Czechs, Russians, Slavs, Bulgarians, Dutch, Hungarians, Germans. What makes it so difficult is that I understand only a few words. Their gratitude tears at my heart when I do something to make them more comfortable or give them a little food or smile at them.

One of the day nurses had a patient that kept leaving his cot and crawling under it to sleep on the bare wooden floor. She decided to put his mattress, sheets and pillow under there too as it seemed to be his favorite place.

The odor from the lack of sanitation over the years makes the whole place smell like rotten, rotten sewage. We wear masks constantly, though they don't keep out the stench. There are commodes in the middle of the room. Patients wear just pajama shirts as they can't get the bottoms down fast enough to use the commodes. God, where are you?

Making rounds by flashlight is an eerie sensation. I'll hear calloused footsteps shuffling behind me and turn in time to see four semi-nude skeletons gliding toward the commodes. God, where were you?

You have to gently shake some of the patients to see if they are still alive. Their breathing is so shallow, pulse debatable. Many die in their sleep. I carry their bodies back to a storage room, they are very light, just the weight of their demineralized bones. Each time, I breathe a wee prayer for them. God, are you there?

In the morning the strongest patients have latrine detail, it takes two of them to carry a commode pail and dump it. They also sweep the floors and carry out the trash. Many patients are only seventeen.

Our men sprayed the camp area to kill the insects that carried many of the diseases. We were told that the SS guards who controlled the camp used to bring a small pan of food into the ward and throw it on the floor. When the stronger patients scrambled for it, like starving beasts, they were lashed with a long whip. It's a corner of hell. Too shocked and tired to write anymore.

Love,

June

—Source: Reprinted by permission of June Wandrey Mann from Bedpan Commando: The Story of a Combat Nurse During World War II by June Wandrey, Elmore Publishing Company, 1946.

JUANITA REDMOND

In September, 1940, Juanita Redmond, a member of the peacetime Army Nurse Corps, arrived in Manila and "floated down the gangplank complete in chiffon dress and an enormous picture hat." Fifteen months later, stunned by the Japanese attack on Pearl Harbor and faced with the imminent invasion of Manila, the U.S. government ordered the medical staff to retreat to the Bataan Peninsula. There the fighting became so intense that the 500-bed hospital they established was soon expanded to care for 1600; nurses coped with the shortage of medical supplies by removing bandages from patents, washing, sterilizing, and reusing them. Food was at a premium: the decision was made that the next step in rationing would limit patients and staff to one meal every other day. Then on Easter Monday, 1942, the hospital took a direct hit. In her book, <u>I Served on Bataan</u>, Redmond describes this harrowing experience. By April 7 it was clear Bataan was going to surrender to the Japanese. Redmond and several other members of the medical staff were evacuated to the labyrinth of rocky passages that comprised the Fortress of Corregidor, an island in Manila Bay. There they continued to treat the wounded in tunnels in temporary safety until Corregidor fell to the Japanese as well.

At ten o'clock on Easter Monday the first wave of bombers struck us.

Someone yelled, "Planes overhead!" But those had become such familiar words that most of us paid them little attention. I went on pouring medications, and then the drone of the planes was lost in the shrill crescendo and roar of a crashing bomb.

It landed at the hospital entrance and blew up an ammunition truck that was passing. The concussion threw me to the floor. There was a spattering of shrapnel and pebbles and earth on the tin roof. Then silence for a few minutes.

I heard the corpsmen rushing out with litters, and I pulled myself to my feet. Precious medicines were dripping to the ground from the shattered dressing carts, and I tried to salvage as much as possible.

The first casualties came in. The boys in the ammunition truck had been killed, but the two guards at the hospital gate had jumped into their fox holes. By the time they were extricated from the debris that filled up the holes they were both shell-shock cases.

There were plenty of others.

Outside the shed a guard yelled, "They're coming back!"

They were after us, all right.

In the Orthopedic ward nurses and corpsmen began to cut the tractgion ropes so that the patients could roll out of bed if necessary, broken bones and all. In my ward several of the men became hysterical; I would have joined them if I could. It was all I could do to go on being calm and acting as if everything were all right and I had everything under control.

"They're very near us!" came the warning from outside.

Father Cummins had come in, and standing in the middle of the shed where all the boys could see him, he asked us to repeat the Lord's Prayer with him.

Then the second wave of bombs fell.

That one hit the mess and the Doctors' and Nurses' Quarters. When the ripping and tearing sound of crashing wood and the roar of minor explosions diminished, I could hear shrieks of pain outside, the helpless sobbing of the men in the wards, and Father Cummins' quiet voice praying.

Through the open sides of the sheds came flying debris, clouds of dust, wrenched boards with protruding nails, limbs of trees.

It wasn't over.

Even in the first few moments of quiet, we heard the planes coming back.

We couldn't do anything but wait. That was the awful part; we couldn't do anything.

This time they scored a direct hit on the wards. A thousand-pound bomb pulverized the bamboo sheds, smashed the tin roofs into flying pieces; the iron beds doubled and broke jaggedly like paper matches. Sergeant May had pulled me under a desk, but the desk was blown into the air, he and I with it.

I heard myself grasping. My eyes were being gouged out of their sockets, my whole body was swollen and torn apart by the violent pressure. This is the end, I thought.

Then I fell back to the floor, the desk landing on top of me and bouncing around drunkenly. Sergeant May knocked it away from me, and gasping for breath, bruised and aching, sick from swallowing the smoke of the explosive, I dragged myself to my feet. I heard Freeman, our boy with no legs, calling out:

"Where's Miss Redmond? Is Miss Redmond alive?"

He was being carried out; fortunately, he had rolled out of bed and, though he had been covered with debris, except for a few scratches he was unhurt.

Father Cummins said calmly: "Somebody take over. I'm wounded." He had shrapnel in his shoulder.

Only one small section of my ward remained standing. Part of the roof had been blown into the jungle. There were mangled bodies under the ruins; a bloodstained hand stuck up through a pile of scrap; arms and legs had been ripped off and flung among the rubbish. Some of the mangled torsos were almost impossible to identify. One of the few corpsmen who had survived unhurt climbed a tree to bring down a body blown into the top branches. Blankets, mattresses, pajama tops hung in the shattered trees.

We worked wildly to get to the men who might be buried, still alive, under the mass of wreckage, tearing apart the smashed beds to reach the wounded and the dead. These men were our patients, our responsibility; I think we were all tortured by an instinctive, irrational feeling that we had failed them.

The bombing had stopped, but the air was rent by the awful screams of the new-wounded and the dying, trees were still crashing in the jungle and when one near by fell on the remaining segment of tin roof it sounded like shellfire. We were shaking and sick at our stomachs, but none of us who was able to go on dared to stop even for a moment.

I saw Rosemary Hogan being helped from her ward. Blood streamed from her face and her shoulder; she looked ghastly.

"Hogan," I called, "Hogan, is it bad?"

She managed to wave her good arm at me. "Just a little nose bleed," she said cheerfully.

That was Hogan, all right. "How about you?"

"I'm okay."

The corpsmen led her off to Surgery, which luckily was still standing.

Then Rita Palmer was taken from her ward. Her face and arms had been cut and her skirt and G.I. shirt had been blown off.

I asked a doctor about the other nurses.

"They're all safe," he said.

But there was no time for thankfulness; we were driven by a terrible urgency to save the twice-wounded patients who were still living; to save the medical aids that would keep them alive.

Kitchen utensils from the destroyed mess were strewn over the grounds. From the shattered Receiving ward case records blew about like confetti. The pharmacy had been hit and most of the drugs were gone, but some cabinets were found to be not too badly smashed and there was a swift desperate search for bottles and boxes that could be salvaged.

Someone yelled that the bombers were coming back, but most of us were simply too battered and too tired to react one way or the other. Some people ran to the fox holes, others just didn't bother.

It was one plane and it circled over us maddeningly: Photo Joe, the Japanese flier who took pictures of struck targets....

With the doctors, each of the nurses on ward-duty made a survey and a record of the living and the dead from her ward. Several of my boys had died of shock; they hadn't been hit, they had been too weak to live through the explosion.

There had been about sixteen hundred beds, or makeshift beds, in our hospital. Now there were only sixty-five left standing. The near-by camps were sending us help, men and supplies, trucks and busses and other vehicles since most of ours were destroyed, and we transferred most of the patients to Hospital No. 2, keeping only those too badly injured to move. Rosemary Hogan and Rita Palmer were taken to Corregidor.

Perhaps I am making this sound as if it all took a long time. It didn't; it was all in the same day of the bombing. And the bombers were still strafing us, though never as they had in the morning. We placed as many patients as we dared near, or even in, the fox holes; but there were those whom it was too dangerous to move and we had to leave them in the beds we had cleaned out in the section of the shed still standing.

The corpsmen tried to make the nurses stay near the fox holes, while they cleaned up the grounds and attended to the patients.

"We can run faster than you can," they said.

However, it was impossible to do much work that afternoon. We waited for darkness and then the entire staff pitched in. We gathered together as many records as we could find and sorted out the wreckage for every scrap of material and supplies that could be salvaged. There were holes to avoid and tin roofing that might collapse at any moment and we had to work by flashlight. We still uncovered arms and legs and mutilated bodies.

That night there were many burials.

Usually the dead were buried as quickly and quietly and reverently as was possible. A grave registration unit was attached to each hospital which attended to all the details and kept the records. We tried not to disturb the other patients in the wards, but the beds were so close that even by moving the deceased patient at night, someone was bound to hear. Night nurses often found that the patient in the next bed had disappeared, especially if he were a Filipino, and was hiding under some other bed. If he stayed in his own bed, he would explain, he would be the next to die.

But this was wholesale burial. We tried not to hear the scraping of the spades or the thud of earth thrown on earth, but we couldn't get away from it. We couldn't be impersonal or detached.

That night we stayed in our fox holes. I didn't sleep. We hadn't eaten since breakfast, but I wasn't hungry. We were like hunted animals, waiting for the kill, almost hoping it would happen quickly so that the torment of waiting would end....

We managed to get together some sort of meal that day, and slowly, under great handicaps, the hospital began to function again. The dressing carts were far from complete, but we made out with what we had as best we could. We concocted many substitutes, rather proud of our ingenuity, and set the Filipinos' clever hands to work making others, such as applicators, for instance, which they made out of stems stripped from the branch of a tree, and then whittled and smoothed into shape.

We wouldn't have been surprised to hear that the hospital site was to be abandoned, but evidently this was not planned, for carpenters were soon busy tacking oilcloth and black paper over the blasted Surgery windows, and we heard that engineers were to be sent out to help us re-establish the hospital.

But that evening of April 7th at six o'clock heavy artillery shells burst through the jungles around our base. Still unknown to us, Bataan was falling. Fort Drum, Fort Hughes, and Corregidor were firing on Bataan beyond our retreating troops, trying to hold back the Japanese forces.

A little over an hour later, the nurses were ordered to be ready to leave in fifteen minutes. There was a bus provided for us, and Captain Nelson would drive down with us to the docks where we would embark for Corregidor.

There was too much to be done and said in so little time. We wanted to discuss certain details about our patients; we wanted to leave careful instructions for the care of those we were particularly worried about; we wanted to know what was happening, why we were being ordered out....

It hurt to say goodbye. All the doctors and corpsmen were there to see us off, and some of them kept saying it wasn't goodbye; in a few days we'd be back again, but nobody believed them. They said it had been good working with us. They said we'd been brave soldiers.

"We'll be seeing you," they all repeated firmly.

—Source: From Chapter VI [pp. 106-122], excerpts totaling 1, 863 words, from I SERVED ON BATAAN by JUANITA REDMOND. Copyright 1943 by Juanita Redmond. Reprinted by permission of HarperCollins Publishers Inc.

4

MILITARY AND ALLIED SERVICE PERSONNEL

The only women to be officially associated with the U.S. military before World War I were nurses who served as auxiliaries to two of the services: the Army Nurse Corps was established in 1901, the Navy in 1908. During World War I, the Navy and the Marines accepted a limited number of enlisted women for duty within the U.S., but these all-female units were quickly disbanded at the conclusion of the war. It was not until World War II created an urgent demand for personnel that women were accepted, begrudgingly at first, in large numbers in the military. General Dwight D. Eisenhower, commander of the Allied Forces in Europe, later admitted, "like most soldiers, I was violently against it."

The Army was the first service to capitulate to the need for more "manpower" by admitting women. Yet, at its inception in May of 1942, the Women's Army Auxiliary Corps was only permitted to grant auxiliary status to its enlistees; military rank, pay, and benefits comparable to those received by the men were withheld. The Navy, Coast Guard, and Marines were slower to accept women, but when they did, the new recruits assumed full military status. This action put pressure on the Army, and the WAAC shed its auxiliary status in September of 1943. The Women's Army Corps served in every theater of operation during the war. Before the conclusion of the war in 1945, almost 400,000 women had served in the combined Armed Services.

It is difficult today to appreciate the emotion and the rhetoric that accompanied this transformation of the military. The conventions of society regarding the roles women could properly fill were deeply embedded in the national consciousness, and most women as well as men felt uncomfortable breaking from traditional norms. Nevertheless, when the call came, thousands of women willingly embraced the unknown, risking censure by others, and performed beyond the expectations of skeptics and supporters alike.

Lt. Col. Mary-Agnes Brown, stationed at Army Headquarters in the Far East, summed up this complex accomplishment:

> ...women in uniform have tactfully carried out a campaign to educate an often-skeptic public in the purpose of women in military service. They have withstood opposition and misunderstandings with a courage which entitles them to a place with other pioneer women who have shaped the course of American history.

Captain Lorena Hermance, a WAC communications officer in North Africa and Italy, reports on General Eisenhower's own change of heart after working with the women assigned to his command:

> ...Gen. Eisenhower said he had been so favorably impressed by the performance of American women in service and has such faith in their capabilities that he has asked to have them placed in every position possible.... he was particularly proud of the WACs who were the "first women to invade No Man's Land."...

Other pioneer women who were buffeted by military and public prejudice but nevertheless performed valuable service with distinction and courage were the Women's Airforce Service Pilots. However, the feasibility of using women pilots in non-combat positions was slow to be accepted. Following prolonged delays, reluctant permission was given Nancy Harkness Love and Jackie Cochran, both experienced pilots in their own right, to experiment with programs using women pilots. Their individual units later combined to form the WASP.

Members of Love's group, the Women's Auxiliary Ferrying Squadron (WAFS), were required to have commercial licenses and 500 hours flight time. After a brief adjustment period, they were assigned to ferry military aircraft from factories to military bases and other points of departure. One of them, Cornelia Fort, makes it clear that the WAFS did not let expressions of doubt, and sometimes derision, from male pilots hamper them in the duty they had chosen:

> That there were men with their tongues in their cheeks goes without saying, men waiting for us to get lost or crack up or prove in some way the undependability of women pilots.... So far, we have done a good job.... We have delivered airplanes, numbers of airplanes, without getting lost and without cracking up.... I have yet to have a feeling which approaches in satisfaction

that of having signed, sealed, and delivered an airplane for the United States Army.

—Simbeck 185–186

Cochran's plan had greater scope. With commercial licenses and a minimum of 200 hours of logged flight time, the Women's Flying Training Detachment (WFTD) members were given classes in weather, navigation, communication, and aircraft mechanics, as well as extensive special flight training. In addition to ferrying, graduates of this program towed targets for antiaircraft trainees, piloted pursuit planes, flew tracking missions, and acted as instructors for Army Airforce pilots in training. Some even took on the essential and dangerous job of test piloting planes which had been repaired or were exhibiting problems. Many male pilots were reluctant to do this testing, feeling that if they were to die in the service of their country, it should be in the throes of battle.

Despite the inherent danger of their work and the dedication shown by the WASP, a bill to grant them full military status failed to pass the Congress in March of 1944. These women served without medical or life insurance or veterans' benefits. In fact, the families of the 38 WASP who died in the service of their country had to pay for their daughters' burial expenses. It was not until November of 1977 that Congress belatedly paid tribute to these women by granting them the benefits given to the male veterans of World War II.

MARY-AGNES BROWN

A World War I nurse wrote to Lt. Col. Mary-Agnes Brown, the WAC staff director at U.S. Army Headquarters in the Pacific, asking about servicewomen in World War II. In her response, Brown shared her perception of the WAC as a social as well as a military force. Her letter articulates the pioneer role of World War II women in uniform, women she believed were transforming society much as their foremothers did a century earlier.

Headquarters, United States Army Forces in the Far East
31 October 1944

Dear Miss Pedersen:

Your letter of 1 October, 1944 has just been received and I am very happy to comment on the subject of "women in service." After two years and a half of Army duty, eight months of which have been spent in Australia and New Guinea, there is much that I would like to say about the types of work women in uniform are performing, the manner in which they are serving, the quick adjustments they have made to military life, and the effect their service will have on women's activities for years to come. Unfortunately, however, limitations of time permit me to make only a brief, general statement.

Women have proved that they can leave the comforts and friendly atmosphere of home for the strange and difficult life of military organization and discipline. They have gladly put aside their individuality in the matter of dress, in exchange for a uniform which places them all on the same democratic level, removing artificial distinctions. They have demonstrated their ability to live well and happily in close proximity to large numbers of other women, mastering the art of "give-and-take" which is the basis of successful communal living. They have brought to their military jobs a wide variety of civilian skills, and performed their duties with the high degree of efficiency, loyalty, and conscientiousness which has characterized women's work in civilian life for many years. Some have acquired new skills which will be of value to them when they return to civilian life.

In addition to their official duties, women in uniform have tactfully carried out a campaign to educate an often-skeptic public in the purpose of women in military service. They have withstood opposition and misunderstandings with a courage which entitles them to a place with other pioneer women who have shaped the course of American history. They have glowed with appreciation of their efforts by those sectors of public opinion which have recognized the need for women in the armed forces.

Service women are truly representative of American womanhood. There are just as many differences in personality, skill, intelligence, and cultural attainments as are to be found among women civilians. When a woman puts on her country's uniform, no radical change occurs. She remains a woman, with feminine instincts and attributes. An extremely small percentage of service women sometimes fall short of the high standard of personal honor and conduct which is expected of all members of the military family, just as in civilian life certain individuals conduct themselves in a manner not generally approved. While these instances are as regrettable as they are rare, they serve to emphasize the high standards and fine qualities of the vast majority. The Army's sensible attitude toward instances of individual failure in duty will undoubtedly affect public opinion which, in the past, has tended to apply a stricter standard of conduct to the female sex. The substitution of a more objective concept, which recognizes women as human beings with their feet on the ground rather than on pedestals, should result in better understanding and improved relations between men and women.

In my opinion the most significant feature of women in service is not that they have made it possible to release thousands of men for combat duty, but that a large percentage of non-combat jobs are more effectively performed by women than men.

An ex-service woman will probably return to civilian life in better physical condition than when she entered service. She will have a wide circle of friends with whom she has intimately shared a great experience. She will be self-reliant and adaptable; eager to find her place in the post-war world. She will be proud of women's war participation throughout the world, both in and out of uniform. She will have an increased sense of civic responsibility, and will actively support women who are taking part in public affairs. She will strive to translate to business, industry, and the professions the Army policy of regarding women as "equal partners" with men.

Most of all, she will be profoundly grateful for the privilege of serving her country and for the sense of satisfaction which comes from playing a small part in a great struggle for personal liberty.

With kindest regards to you and appreciation of the splendid services you and other members of the Army Nurse Corps rendered in World War I, which have been a constant inspiration to women of World War II, I am

Sincerely yours,

Mary-Agnes Brown

—Source: "Letter, October 31, 1944," by Lt. Col. Mary-Agnes Brown in <u>With Love, Jane: Letters from American Women on the War Fronts,</u> ed. Alma Lutz, The John Day Company, 1945 in the Archives of John Day Company, Department of Rare Books and Special Collections, Princeton University Library.

VERA HAMERSCHLAG

Late in 1942, the Coast Guard realized its need for a women's reserve. Known as SPARS, these women brought technical as well as administrative skills to positions in intelligence, engineering and communications.

In the summer of 1943, it was decided that SPARS should take over the operation of all Loran Monitor Stations within the continental U.S. Loran was a highly classified scientific development of World War II which used radio signals at stationary locations to aid ships and planes in calculating their exact location. In the following selection, we hear the first hand account of Lt. Vera Hamerschlag, who commanded the operation and was responsible for the technical maintenance of a Loran monitor station on Cape Cod staffed solely by SPARS.

In the summer of 1943, Headquarters decided that Loran Monitor Stations within [the] continental United States should be manned by Spars. Loran is one of those alphabet names meaning Long Range Aid to Navigation—a system developed at the beginning of the war whereby radio signals, transmitted from two shore-based stations, are picked up by a certain type of receiver-indicator installed in ships and planes, enabling them to calculate their exact position. The monitor station is equipped with the same type of receiver-indicator, but being a fixed station, is able to check the accuracy and general operations of the transmitting stations. The Spar operators had to stand watch 24 hours a day, taking and recording these measurements every two minutes.

Having worked as an assistant to the Naval Liaison Officer for Loran at Radiation Lab and thereby becoming familiar with the Loran System, I was selected to be in charge of the first Spar monitor station at Chatham, Massachusetts. One enlisted Spar and I were assigned to a two months' course at M.I.T. in Loran operation and maintenance of receiving equipment. We were the only women in the whole Loran section of the Naval Training School and, needless to say, caused comment. Later, 10 enlisted Spars were assigned to a one-week course in operations only. The selection of these Spars was unique to say the least. Loran was so "hush-hush" that not even the Training Officer had any conception of what the duties of these Spars would be, nor what their qualifications should be. The Engineering Officer had laconically said: "Ability to keep their mouths shut." Thus, all Spars selected were volunteers who had accepted the assignment with a spirit of adventure. It was the first time that Spars were being sent out of the district office and the newness and mystery of the work was a challenge to us all.

At the time I reported, Unit 21 was manned 100 percent by men and the idea was for them to leave for overseas assignments as quickly as we were capable of taking over. We did this within one month—100 percent Spars with the exception of one male radio technician who was a veritable 'man Friday' to us all. He acted as instructor as well, and left six months later when we felt qualified to accept the responsibility of technical maintenance.

The station consisted of one small building about 50 feet long and 30 feet wide. This provided sleeping quarters, recreation room, office space, operations room, repair shop and storage space! I had arrived in advance purposely to get the hang of operations on the spot and additional technical information, but in actuality the whole week was spent in 'setting up housekeeping,' trying to make this small space accommodate 12 Spars and all their gear. Little had I realized when I was told I would be commanding officer of a Loran monitor station how many angles it involved. I was operations and engineering officer, medical officer, barracks officer, personnel officer, training officer—and even Captain of the Head! I had to learn the intricacies of plumbing, of a coal furnace, of a Kohler engine that supplied emergency power when the main line was out—and being on the Cape where nor'easters are frequent, the times were many. I remember the feeling I had when I looked at the 125' mast for the station's antenna and wondered which Spar would climb the riggin' if something went wrong. I asked the CO whom I was replacing who took care of it. His nonchalant answer was not to worry since nothing would happen to it short of a hurricane. Well, we had that too the following fall during which operations were suspended and all hands evacuated in case the mast should topple over onto the buildings!

Well, after a week of planning night and day for the arrival of the Spars, preparing barrack regulations, watch-standing schedules (which resulted in four hours on and eight off due to the nature of the duties, with a '48' every six days and a '72' every eighteen days), contacting the chaplain, the USO, the laundry, ordering supplies and feeling very much more like a housekeeper than a CO, I went down in the Lighthouse truck to meet the first contingent of Spars coming from Boston on the morning train. Our arrival on the Cape was at the worst time of the year—January. All was bleak and lonely, but oh—so white and clean! The station was located right on the water's edge at the show place of the town, about a mile from Main Street. In front was a vast expanse of white sand and beyond, the Atlantic. I shall never forget the hypnotic beauty of the moonbeams on the water, the slowly revolving light from the Lighthouse and the small sentinel light on our antenna mast, combining to make our station a bit of fairyland.

The esprit de corps of Unit 21 was outstanding. We were a family unit. I remember the church wedding we had for one of our members. I gave the bride away, the chaplain performed the ceremony in the local church, and all the townspeople turned out for it!

The human element of the work kept it from getting dull and routine for the operators. The thought that we were participating in a system that was playing such an important part in winning the war gave us a feeling of being as close to the front lines as it was possible for Spars to be. Furthermore, we were part of a network that covered nearly all the world where we or our allies were fighting.

Inasmuch as Loran is considered one of the outstanding scientific developments of this war, it is a satisfaction to know that Spars were given the opportunity to participate in its operation.

The unit at Chatham is believed to have been at that time the only all-female manned one of its kind in the world. A Headquarters letter of commendation stated: "...the operation of Unit 21 under the Spars has been carried out in a most efficient manner and the efforts of the Spar personnel have contributed greatly to the overall efficiency of the Loran system during World War II."

—Source: <u>Three Years Behind the Mast: The Story of the United States Coast Guard SPARS</u>, by Mary C. Lyne and Kay Authur, United States Coast Guard, 1946.

DOROTHY SCHWARTZ

A frequently recurring theme in the diaries and letters of the women actively engaged in war work is patriotism. One of the clearest and most extended descriptions of that powerful motivating force was written as a private letter by WAC Sgt. Dorothy Schwartz, a Hunter College graduate who served in England in 1943 and later in Belgium. She expresses the satisfaction of being wanted and needed by her country and the knowledge that her service has increased her own tolerance, self-discipline and unselfish commitment to the welfare of others.

England (1943)

Dear -------

It is close to 0400, Army time; in anybody's time, when life is at its lowest ebb. I'm not writing because I'm unable to sleep. I'm writing during a pause in my work, for my shift is from midnight to 0730, and I'm writing because of a real desire to talk to you. This is the only way it can be done, for we are thousands of miles apart and I can't call you over the phone and hear your low, clear voice reaching me across the miles...But as I can see you so well in your letters, I know you can read into these lines my own facial expressions, my movements, my very tones, and that you will understand full well what I am trying to say.

I don't know what it is like outside since I came on duty, for my job is to stick at this desk no matter what happens and not leave it. But probably it is deep, dark night with heavy, low clouds, and the thick mist which obscured everything more than a foot away is still burdening the earth...England! Even now, when the initial excitement has long since passed off, when we have been here long enough to have settled down completely—even now, I say, to use "England" as a return address is still startling at times. And how I revel in this piece of fortune! To be able to visualize myself finally and easily as the woman behind the man behind the gun—could any dream come true be more satisfying?...

…. No inspiration in labor is quite similar to that of "being wanted," and with that inspiration our ardor and zeal were so great as to be almost volcanic. Those of us with previous training and experience, stenographers, typists, telephone operators, all took these new positions quite in our stride; those who had to be trained made admirable students; all of us were conscientiously earnest. Our worth was gratefully acknowledged at once. Army and civilian jobs are not comparable, and the civilian job offers the individual more latitude in every direction, but that's not what the Army is for. The Army requires that a job be done and be done it must if we are to win wars.

But this is something I discovered not long ago. There is no advantage in war except what the individual makes for himself. In the Army we lose eccentricities, prejudices, pettiness, because they cannot survive in the face of matter-of-factness and non-luxurious living. We lose the intolerances built upon ignorance and, believe me, there is not one of us who is not a better woman because of it, too. Most people will acquire some degree of tolerance and self-discipline, both of which are seldom deliberately fostered in civilian life and both of which will forever stand us in good stead. Some will be broadened by travel and meeting many people. Others will concentrate upon the social life wherever they are.

The essentials of good character or individual personality are never lost. An expert craftsman can mold clay, chip stone, or fashion wood all to the same size and pattern without changing the essential characteristics of each material. And so with people of any Army group. They can be dressed alike, fed the same food, exposed to the same experiences, but no two will emerge with the same reactions. This individuality the Army cannot destroy—nor does it seek to do so. Its sole interest is to obtain from each a required reaction to a stimulus, which collective response is designed to lead to victory. But the concepts of duty and service are our greatest acquisitions. The whys and wherefores of existence itself undergo serious consideration, and the importance to self and society of unselfish living is rated higher and higher.

How thoroughly noble that sounds, doesn't it? It reads like a political tract, doesn't it? Maybe you'll think I'm trying to sell someone a bill of goods. Or maybe you'll think I'm trying to sell *myself* a bill of goods. Well, if it sounds noble, don't cheapen it or sneer at it.... If it reads like a political tract, make the most of it. American women are way behind the women of England, Russia or China when it comes to unselfish service to their nation, and so ultimately to unselfish devotion to their own homes. If you think I'm trying to sell someone a bill of goods, forget it. She'd probably sicken early anyway at plowing through mud or "sweating out" the few hot water sessions during the day or the lack of fresh milk and eggs and fruit or the continuous sameness of the khaki uniform or the long hours of hard work or the nightly blackout vigilance.

I don't have to sell myself. I had a chance to leave the Corps. It would have been easy to return to the family, friendships, luxury, accustomed routines, and habits of former life. Not so much time had been lost that I could not move easily into the old niches. But I had other ideas, and have them still. I'm becoming a more tolerant woman, a more conscientious citizen with truer ideals of duty and corresponding privilege.

Maybe a lot of Wacs wouldn't say it quite that way; maybe a lot of Wacs wouldn't say it at all; but a lot of Wacs are sure thinking it!

Dorothy

—Source: "Letter, England (1943)," by Dorothy Schwartz in <u>With Love, Jane: Letters from American Women on the War Fronts</u>, ed. Alma Lutz, The John Day Company, 1945 in the Archives of John Day Company, Department of Rare Books and Special Collections, Princeton University Library.

LORENA HERMANCE

The first grandmother to join the WACs, Lorena Hermance, signed up at age 44, a year under the limit, to contribute her telephone communication skills to the war effort. Although expecting to be posted near her California home, she found herself an officer at Eisenhower's headquarters in Algiers, in charge of the largest communications network in North Africa. Her job was often one of improvisation, trouble shooting, and diplomacy as she dealt with communications breakdowns, antiquated equipment and the integration of staff from several nations.

The experience of surmounting such challenges was useful in her next assignment as Wires Traffic Officer for the Allied Forces during the Italian Campaign in 1944–45. The first and only woman to serve with the 50 male American and British officers in the Allied Forces Signal Section, she was charged with inspecting all the switchboard installations in Italy, "from Naples to the front lines [and] from the Mediterranean to the Adriatic Seas." When the war ended, the British made her an M.B.E., Member of the British Empire; the Americans awarded her the Bronze Star for "meritorious achievement in connection with military operations."

The following entry is taken from the diary she kept for her granddaughter.

There is so much to learn that we must cram endlessly. We have tests each day and study until lights out at night. It has been such a long long time since I was a school girl that I have lost the knack of proper study. It has not been easy for me. I seem unable to retain knowledge simply by reading a text and need to discuss it with someone....

The course I was taking was supposed to be completed in eight weeks. At the end of five I was ordered by the company commander to appear before the OCS (Officer Candidate School) board.

Most of the girls are extremely nervous about appearing before the board. They sit in the corridor awaiting their turn in anxiety and apprehension. I have still not managed to convince myself that I want to be an officer so I suppose it didn't matter quite so much to me what was beyond that closed door. Actually it was an ordeal a trifle like what one would expect a police interrogation to be. I was seated before three WAAC officers, facing the window with the light in my eyes. I couldn't see their faces very well. I took a deep breath, sat up straight and silently vowed that no matter how brutally they third-degree'd me, I would not reveal where the body was buried.

I got along pretty well until they began to quiz me on current events. For the life of me I couldn't remember things, particularly dates and events pertinent to our entry into the war! They queried me endlessly on how I would handle this or that situation; how I would administer problems which might be distasteful to me or regulations or controversial subjects. I kept answering and peering at them, trying to get a good look at them, to see whether they looked as if they thought I was stupid as I thought I sounded. At last it was over. I felt like I'd been through the eye of a hurricane. I plastered a bright confident smile on my face in the hope it might encourage the others awaiting their turn. I tried. I honestly did. Maybe it's just the traditional female perversity. I'm not sure I want to be an officer but I'm darned if I want it on my record that I'm too stupid to be one!

I've passed and been chosen as an OCS candidate....

◆ ◆ ◆

I realize that because WAAC is in its formative stages and officer material is as yet scarce, some of us are being "walked up the ladder" quite rapidly. I am aware too, that only those who are considered by our superiors to show "marked capabilities" are being chosen; it is a source of considerable pride and encouragement to me that I am obviously in that group. It imposes, on the other hand, considerable obligation and a continued sense of tension, since more must obviously be required of us in a short time than will be exacted from those who follow later. They will be permitted a normal length of training and time in which to absorb all these new duties and the precise meaning and significance of each. I most earnestly desire to fulfill my obligations adequately and feel somehow I will be able to do this....

Most of the officers are under thirty and have no home ties.... I have promised Bill [her husband] that I will not volunteer for overseas. Mine may not be the most exciting corner of this war but there is obviously a great deal to be done here so I shall stay at home and do it. There is a possibility of my being assigned but considering my age it is entirely unlikely, actually only enlisted women have a choice. Officers go where ordered....

◆ ◆ ◆

Out of the whole regimental group, in which I was the only one who did not request overseas duty—guess who is going overseas....

I received my orders today. The old involuntary volunteer, Lorena. I simply don't know whether to laugh or cry.

I have been assigned to the 190th Communications Company. The first WAC communications group to be formed and sent into field training.

…. I am informed that I was chosen because of my background in telephone communications. The TO (Table of Organizations) which is the Bible concerning number of officers and enlisted women required for each section was filled from company personnel wherever they were, if they had the necessary qualifications for the job at hand. I am assigned as platoon commander and will be operations officer when we reach our ultimate destination wherever that may be.

Later, in Algiers…

We have begun orientation classes and tours of signal centers, preparing to take them over and release the men who are badly needed at the front lines. The largest switchboard serving the armed forces in our theater is <u>Freedom</u>….

◆ ◆ ◆

I have girls on the Algiers long distance board, a small Red Cross installation, some on detached service in Oran and Constantine and a fair sized board under command of the British Eighth Army Group located on the outskirts of Algiers. Our telephone slogan is "Let Freedom Ring"….

Not all the equipment is as modern as Freedom, by any means, but the girls are doing an excellent job with all equipment. Some is so obsolete that I have had to make a study of it myself before instructing my operators in its use. This is particularly true of the antiquated French equipment.

Our tours of duty are around the clock. Day sleeping is a bit difficult in so large a company. Some of the girls can even sleep through a shelling but others cannot. We have fixed up a small inside, top-floor room which is kept darkened for those who need isolated rest.

Our OSS (Office of Strategic Services) board and installation are so top secret that everyone who passes through this enclosure must have a special pass, after having had an exhaustive security check even though this had been done once just before our departure from the States. Needless to say, I have assigned girls to this job who can be implicitly trusted with the highly critical information they handle….

General Ike (Eisenhower) has his offices on the second floor of HQ's. It is the highlight of a day, to officers and enlisted women alike, if we meet him on the stairs or in a corridor. He always has a cheery greeting, along with that wonderful impish grin of his. The girls idolize him.

I have been ordered to choose one of my subordinates and eight enlisted personnel to send to Cairo to handle the switchboard for the private use of the conference between President Roosevelt, Winston Churchill and Chiang Kai Chek. I have assigned Lt. Grace Smith to the detail and given her eight girls capable of working around the clock and completely dependable when in charge of important communications....

Received orders to take several telephone girls to Oran.... On the return trip from Oran to Algiers we ran into a swarm of locusts. I could hardly credit my senses. The creatures were so thick they blotted out the sun like a cloud. We could move at a pace no more than five miles an hour. The road was so covered that my driver could hardly see where he was going and driving over the things made the road mud-slick so that the truck kept skidding and slipping. The locusts were devouring crops and everything in their path. Frantic Arabs in the field were beating on tin, waving their arms, screaming and trying futilely to drive them away....

Later, in Italy...

My job as Wires Traffic Officer for Allied Forces seems to grow more demanding by the day. I have all the brass right here in the building ready to jump on me for the least minor infraction by any personnel under my supervision. The British seem the most difficult to please.

We are working under stringent conditions and when the pressure is put on me to get a job done all I can do is pressure my operators in turn and to try for perfect performance out of what equipment we have working. It is a vastly greater job and challenge than the one in North Africa. It is important that we iron out the problems immediately and get control of the situation....

Beside the big Freedom board, I have all the smaller installations in the outlying areas. The equipment, mostly of French or Italian design, is all obsolete, usually in poor working condition and extremely difficult to service.

Enlisted men are assigned here too. They do not, especially, like switchboard work. With Italian civilian girls, ATS (British servicewomen), G.I.'s and WACs under my supervision, I really have my hands full. We work in shifts around the clock.

This is the first time in military history that women have been given such important work to do. I am determined that Allied Forces will have nothing but the highest commendation for the Freedom telephone girls or any of the personnel working under my direction....

The problems that confront me each day never leave my mind. Even though we have a modern Stromberg-Carlson board, it was never meant to carry the heavy load of traffic that comes through these headquarters. I have to improvise and along with some ingenuity this keeps the mind working on the job and off. Asleep or awake I seem to be figuring some way to overcome our shortage of materials needed. We have a bigger challenge than what I expected...

We now have 15 companies of WACs in Italy, stationed in Naples, Florence, Bari, Sienna, Rome and Leghorn. One is with Fifth Army Forward and seven in Caserta....

◆ ◆ ◆

I have been given an assignment which is both extremely important and challenging. I am being transferred into AFHQ Signal Section; the first woman ever directly assigned to them. We have, of course, been working under their jurisdiction but assigned to a company of the WAC battalion. I will be the only woman in a group of 50 male officers. The reason for the transfer is that I've been chosen by both American and British command in AFHQ to represent American Signal installations, Allied Forces and to tour the whole of Italy inspecting all major and some minor switchboard installations from Naples to the front lines [and] from the Mediterranean to the Adriatic Sea. I am to be accompanied by a British officer, Captain J. D. Rollings, Traffic Officer (Philpot) of the 15th Army Group. He will take his batman, a car and driver. These (car and driver) I will be responsible for since they are from our motor pool.

I am tremendously complimented at having been given this assignment. I cannot help wondering what the reaction of the British officer will be. It's so obvious that the male officers, American and British, are annoyed to see a woman given so much responsibility. Some of them have given me a pretty hard time....

◆ ◆ ◆

We found a bad situation in Bari. They had WAC operators here with G.I.'s supervising. Any one of the girls here knows far more than their supervisors about the work for they have been trained and are giving excellent performances. They have been continually clashing with the men who apparently consider it beneath their dignity to yield to any form of female superiority. Morale here was low. I don't think it will take long to straighten the situation out....

◆ ◆ ◆

What a day! When we reached the installation here [Sienna, Italy], I was informed that Headquarters wished me to call them at once on a most urgent matter. I thought, Oh, Lord, what had happened now? I got Lt. Woolf, my officer in charge, on the wire. She said,

"Just a moment, General Back wishes to speak to you".

(He is my immediate superior, having replaced General Tully. I consider him one of the finest gentlemen I have ever met.)

He came on the wire and I said a bit apprehensively,

"Lieutenant Hermance reporting, Sir".

"Lieutenant Hermance," he roared at me. "I don't know <u>any</u> such person. I know a <u>Captain</u> Hermance. How are you, Captain?

And that, my dears, is how "Grandma" received word of her promotion. Even if I had dreamed of it, I would not have expected it to happen so soon after my being transferred to an all-male section….

◆ ◆ ◆

Back in Caserta. A few loose ends must be tied up at Naples before we can call our assignment complete and Capt. Rollings and I can start compiling our official report. We have covered 2500 miles and inspected 52 switchboards under adverse conditions all along the way. The experience was well worth the hardships. Now for the proof of the pudding. All this has to be compiled as it will be the nucleus for the new SOP (Standard Order of Procedure) for all theaters of war for use in wires communications.

Capt. Rollings and I have worked for four days continuously writing from our notes. Now they will have to be typed and sent up to the powers that be. I am physically and mentally burned out….

◆ ◆ ◆

5 May 1945, Germans surrender unconditionally in Northwestern Germany, Holland and Denmark. The only organized resistance left includes remnants of an army in Czechoslovakia, the corner of northeastern Austria and a few pockets on the east front along the Atlantic coast of France and the garrison of Norway.

Our status on Freedom at this point is 67 Satellite boards, 235 trunk lines, 1126 local lines, 22 positions and 296 recorded long distance calls with a record high peg-count of calls for one day of 38,430. This is more calls than some cities handle for public service.

Back on the job and plenty of work awaiting for me. Got an early start this morning as I wanted a briefing from Lt. Ida Woolf, whom I had assigned to take over while I was away. She told me that on 7 May, the Germans' unconditional surrender was announced at AFHQ. The place went wild with ticker and teletype tape thrown from the windows, waste baskets emptied into the courtyard and Freedom board lit up like a torch. They were worried that the overload would blow all the fuses. All maintenance men were standing by!....

◆ ◆ ◆

The Meritorious Service Unit citation was awarded the 2666 WAC Wires Co.... This is the culmination of my hopes and their efficiency on the job. It is a well earned honor....

On 29 July, [1945] orders were issued awarding me the M.B.E., Member of the British Empire. This honor came as a complete surprise. I felt it a tremendous privilege to be awarded this medal which comparatively few Americans have received. I have received the ribbon from General Nalder but the medal itself is to be presented in a formal ceremony. Impressive engraved invitations have been sent out by the Field Marshall's American aide to all the top British and American brass in Signals and to many of my friends, officers from General Nalder's and General McNarney's camp and the WAC Battalion....

Greatly honored as I felt at the recognition bestowed upon me by the British Empire, I think the high point of my military career and the moment which will always burn most brightly in my memory came today. It was completely unexpected and without pomp or circumstance.

In a very brief informal ceremony in the office of General George I. Back, Chief Signal Officer, MTOUSA, who read and presented the award on the recommendation of the male officers with whom I have worked for the past two years; I was awarded the Bronze Star for "meritorious achievement in connection with military operations".

Me, the gal whose intense inner urging prompted enlistment and would have served the three years willingly scrubbing latrines if that was to have been my lot. I can hardly believe that all these high honors are being given to me!"

I think that no achievement of mine, no honor won, will ever give me the feeling of intense pride and gratification that I am experiencing in this gesture by fine men who laid aside all personal prejudice against "petticoat soldiers" and accepted me on my merits as an officer and a human being.

I do not recall, save in a general sense, the words of the British citation but these of Major Warren (Rags) Ragland, Group Wires Officer, who instigated the award, I could virtually recite from memory:

> ...The high quality of telephone service furnished Allied Force Headquarters during the period July 1944, to August 1945 was largely due to the inspiring leadership and superior organizational ability of Captain Hermance. The entire record of her achievements in the Mediterranean Theater of Operations constitutes a noteworthy example of inspiring devotion to duty which contributed greatly to the successful operation of Allied Forces Headquarters.

—Source: "As You Were," t.s. 1942–1945, Lorena Estelle Hermance Papers, Sophia Smith Collection, Smith Collection, Northampton, MA.

CORNELIA FORT

When Japanese planes struck Pearl Harbor, a 22-year-old pilot, Cornelia Fort, was flying over Honolulu, giving a lesson to a defense worker. In the following account, Fort registers the shock and disbelief she felt on discovering that the military plane bearing down on her small two-seater was painted with the Rising Sun, symbol of Imperial Japan.

.... Just prior to the last landing I was going to have him make before soloing, I looked casually around and saw a military plane coming in from the sea. We were so used to military traffic and our respective safety zones that I merely noted his position subconsciously and nodded for my student to make his turn onto the base leg of the traffic pattern.

I then turned to look around to see if we were clear to make the last turn into the field and saw the other airplane coming directly toward me and at my altitude. I jerked the controls away from my student and jammed the throttle wide open to pull above the oncoming plane.

I remember a distinct feeling of annoyance that the Army plane had disrupted our traffic pattern and violated our safety zone. He passed so close under us that our celluloid windows rattled violently, and I looked down to see what kind of plane it was.

The painted red balls on the tops of the wings shone brightly in the sun. I looked again with complete and utter unbelief. Honolulu...was familiar with the emblem of the Rising Sun on passenger ships but not on airplanes.

I looked quickly at Pearl Harbor, and my spine tingled when I saw billowing black smoke. Still I thought hollowly it might be some kind of coincidence or maneuvers. It might be, it must be. For surely, dear God....

Then I looked way up and saw formations of silver bombers riding in. I saw something detach itself from a plane and come glistening down. My eyes followed it down, down, and even with knowledge pounding in my mind, my heart turned over convulsively when the bomb exploded in the middle of the Harbor.

Most people wonder how they would react in a crisis; if the danger comes as suddenly as this did you don't have time to be frightened. I'm not brave, but I knew the air was not the place for our little baby airplane and I set about landing as quickly as ever I could. It was as if the attack was happening in a different time track, with no relation to me.

I was doubtless a little authoritative when I arrived at the hangar and said in a voice creaking with excitement, "The Japs are attacking," but I was unprepared for their disbelieving laughter and their dismissal of the whole thing as some sort of maneuvers. I didn't stop to think that they were trying to deny it as long as possible, a natural form of wishful thinking, but with the danger gone for me, at least momentarily, I suddenly reacted in anger. I was damn good and mad that they didn't believe me. Just as I was about to protest, a mechanic ran up from a lower hangar and said hoarsely, "That strafing plane that just flew over killed Bob Tyce." [Airport manager Tyce, flying in a Cub with a student, had landed hurriedly and was killed as he ran toward the hangars.] I looked at him in horror and my scalp prickled. I knew bullets aimed at me had killed a friend.

Suddenly that little wedge of sky above Hickam and Pearl Harbor was the busiest, fullest piece of sky I ever saw.... Our antiaircraft started belching shells which left their puffs of smoke scattered like so many umbrellas floating thru the air, planes darting in and out, high and low. One came screaming down in flames, leaving a crimson wake; the detonation of the bombs bursting shook the ground under us.

Cornelia Fort joined the Women's Auxiliary Ferrying Squadron (WAFS) at its inception in 1942. Mindful of the danger of the times, before she left Honolulu for the mainland she wrote her mother a letter in which she endeavored to describe her joy in life, her love of flying. Little more than a year later, she died at the controls of her plane, the first woman pilot in U.S. history to lose her life in the line of duty.

> I want you to know that except for not seeing you in the last weeks when I've ached for you so, my life has been exceedingly happy. Thanks to the environment, both physical and spiritual, that you and Dad gave me, my life has been rich and full of meaning.
>
> I've loved the green pastures and the cities, the sunshine on the plains, and the rain in the mountains. Springtime in New York and fog in San Francisco.
>
> Books and music have been deeply personal things to me, possessions of the soul. I've loved the multitudinous friends in many places and their many kindnesses to me. I've loved the steak and red wine and dancing in smoky nightclubs, self-important headwaiters who bring the reams of French bread and wine sauces in New Orleans. I've loved the ice coldness of the air in the Canadian Laurentians, the camaraderie of skiing, and the first scotch and soda as you sit in front of the fire....
>
> I dearly loved the airports, little and big. I loved the sky and the planes, and yet, best of all, I loved flying. For it too was a deeply personal possession of the soul. I loved Johnny [Koons], because he knew what I meant when we were fly-

ing and I suddenly grinned or clapped my hands because the inside excitement was too great not to grin.

I loved it best perhaps because it taught me utter self-sufficiency, the ability to remove myself beyond the keep of anyone at all—and in so doing it taught me what was of value and what was not.

It taught me a way of life—in the spiritual sense. It taught me to cherish dignity and integrity and to understand the importance of love and laughter.

For I have loved many people and many places and many things, and best of all I have loved life, and especially American life. And if I can say one thing in truth, it is that to my friends and my convictions I have brought all the loyalty and integrity of which I was capable.

If I die violently, who can say it was "before my time"? I should have dearly loved to have had a husband and children. My talents in that line would have been pretty good, but if that is not to be, I want no one to grieve for me.

I was happiest in the sky—at dawn when the quietness of the air was like a caress, when the noon sun beat down, and at dusk when the sky was drenched with the fading light. Think of me there and remember me, I hope, as I shall you.

With love,

Cornelia

—Source: "Letters, December 1941, January 1942," in <u>Daughter of the Air: The Brief Soaring Life of Cornelia Fort</u> by Rob Simbeck, copyright 1999, by permission of Grove/Atlantic, Inc.

WASP

The Women's Airforce Service Pilots shared Cornelia Fort's passion for flying. The following excerpts from their letters reveal the exhilaration experienced by these pilots as well as their implicit acceptance of the peril inherent in the work they have chosen. In the first three sets of letters, written while in training at Avenger Field in Sweetwater, Texas, Marjorie Osborne, Madge Rutherford, and Mary Anna Martin share their personal experiences: their moments of doubt and anxiety, their triumphs and joy, as they learn to fly "the Army way."

MARJORIE OSBORNE—CLASS 44-W-9

May 20, 1944

Oh, you poor darling earth-bound people! You have no idea of the thrill of flying a PT—how do you live? You don't, you merely exist.

Well, I passed my first civilian check today. Mr. Hampsmire, W-9's flight commander, was the lucky man! He is a darling—a gruff old guy who looks as though he'd bite your ears off, but is really as sweet as he can be underneath, if you do what he tells you to, with a "Yes, sir!" After leaving the traffic pattern he asked me to climb to 5400' (indicated-2400' ground) to do stalls. I did three normal stalls—one straight ahead, one to the right and left, and three rudder exercise, ditto. He then asked for a spin, so I did tow turns and made a not-so-good recovery. He explained how the recovery should be, then grinned and asked if I could do a chandelle! I gulped and shook my head—(we aren't s'posed to have shandelles until 35 hours.) He did a few for me and then asked me to do two, one something <u>new</u>! A forced landing from 400' which I executed very nicely, back to the field when I did him a beautiful landing, and that was all there was to it. When I told my instructor about the chandelles, he burst out laughing, "Well, if he was showing you chandelles, you were all right!" Later on, after he'd talked to Mr. Hampsmire, he told me that the only criticism was that I corrected too much for torque on my climbing turns....

May 27
Glenn, Texas

…. Yesterday I took off from the auxiliary field to go out to the area to practice maneuvers. There were storm clouds to the south of us and as I "revved" up, Mr. Hampsmire, the flight commander who gave me my check ride, came up to the plane and told me that if it looked any worse while I was flying I should head for home, the main field—Avenger, and land instead of coming back to Aux.#2. As soon as I had reached an altitude of 500' I realized that it was worse than it had looked on the ground, so I headed for the main field. By the time I reached it a dust storm had completely covered the field and probably would have meant plowing into one of the hangars or other planes had I attempted to land there. So back to Aux.#2 I went, but it was covered by the dust storm so that I couldn't even see it. I headed north to get out of the area covered by the dust storm and looking back I saw the most unusual sight! I was completely in the clear—sunshine and warmth all around me, while in back of me along a huge front came this dust storm just billowing red dust. I didn't realize the immensity of it until I started to climb to see if I could get above it. I climbed to 7000' (actual, not indicated—indicated was 9400'—remember, 2400 ground level here), turned back heading south and was met by clouds of dust and high winds. I turned back out of it and headed east keeping north of the dust front. At long last I reached the eastern end of it and went around it, finally going straight west again. As I went west I kept getting into the sand and dust more and more until I was in the middle of the storm again and couldn't see 3 ft. ahead of me or the ground. So north I went and finally gained on the storm. I was so glad to be out of it because while I was in the storm vainly looking for the field so that I could land, the gusts were so strong there were times when I was out of control of the plane.

I kept heading north until I was well ahead of the sand storm and by that time I was out of gas and had to land in this oat field. I made a good landing and the plane is in good shape. A farmer saw me land, took me to a grocery store about 1 ½ miles away where I called the field collect and talked to operations. He, Captain Taylor, gave me my orders which were to employ someone to guard the plane all night and find someplace to stay for the night and not to give any information or let any pictures be taken. He was very nice and told me not to worry—they'd send someone for me in the morning….

Sept. 2, 1944

…. Last night after we'd all landed, we noticed an AT-6 that kept circling and circling the field. We went up into the control tower to find out what was wrong, and the control tower operator was giving the girl instructions on how to get her gear down. The poor kid had been up for two hours, the last hour having been spent trying to get the landing gear down. She did everything—power dives, snap rolls, loops, lazy eights—all over the field so that the tower could tell her if her gear came down—you see, those maneuvers get jammed gear loose sometimes. Finally after a vertical reverse that had us all gasping, the gear came down, but wouldn't lock.

Well, by that time everybody was on the flight line watching her and hoping she'd get in before it got dark—she's a W-10 and never had had night flying. One of the army captains ordered the ambulance and the crash truck out to the runway in case the gear should buckle when she hit the ground. We all held our breaths as she came in for a perfect three point and it was so gentle that the gear stayed down. Whew—then we all went home and ate supper in peace—what a day…

—Source: "Letters, May 20, 27 and September 2, 1944," by Marjorie Osborne by permission of the Woman's Collection, Texas Woman's University.

MADGE RUTHERFORD—CLASS 43-W-4

Tuesday-Post-mess
[4/7/43]

Dearest Mother & Dad:

.... I wish you could have seen the landscape as I saw it yesterday from 6500 feet. As the lower air stratus were much too bumpy for successful low works and I didn't need any more duel on Lazy 8's and chandelles, [Instructor] Jones and I went cloud-hopping. There was a cumulus overcast at 5000–5500 feet, scattered cottony blobs and we went merrily up and over and down and under like a roller-coaster. Then I received some legitimate instruction on slow rolls, snap-rolls, and loops (which I have been practicing solo without instruction) and was complimented on my works. Then I was given off-the-record demonstration of vertical snap rolls and inverted zooms, all very much fun. After we got tired of such childish playing, we went downstairs and chased whirl-winds, tall columns of dust like small tornadoes which the wind spins up from the Texas terrain and which travel exactly like tornadoes and have, in small degree, the same effect. There was an ulterior motive to this since any pilot down here must learn to recognize these and know how it feels to be caught in one so he will react properly. Hitting one during take-off means a sure crack-up....

Love,

Madge

6/5/43

Dearest Mother & Dad:

Yesterday, the last period, from 4:45 to 6:00, I was upstairs, riding the front on a buddy ride with Fran Rohrer under the hood. We were about 1,500 feet above overcast which rode the winds at the 7,000 foot level. After about 40 minutes of turns and courses, me keeping my eyes peeled for other ships and telling her when her turns were too steep, I had her let down to below the overcast. We were about eight miles east of Sweetwater, and when I turned to my left I saw the granddaddy of all dust storms moving rapidly across the plateaus toward Lake Sweetwater. It was the vanguard of some of the most cobalt cloud formation I've ever seen. I yelled to Rohrer to come out from under and take a look.

She did and, on the inter phone, told me that it was my baby. I shoved the mixture of full rich, and assumed a power glide of 140 per. The air was rough as a corduroy road and when I began to slow down and level off at 500 feet, I felt like I was flying a butter churn. After getting a clearance to enter traffic from the oh so anxious tower, I turned on my base leg, let down to 100 feet and made a power approach and wheel landing. Just as I got the flaps rolled up and was taxiing straight ahead rapidly to get out of the way, the storm hit the field and visibility was zero. I waited until I could see, barely, and then crept on up to the edge of the field where I turned and fought all controls of the ship in some of the fanciest cross-wind taxiing you ever hope to see, and I ever hope to do. I suppose I stopped at least five certain ground loops, and eased the ship into the front line without any damage being done. The uncertainty of taxiing can best be illustrated by the fact that Maintenance sent trucks out to tow in the other ships which began to land as soon as the dust storm had passed and the clouds were tolling in. My flight instructor and ex-flight instructor met me at the parachute room, both highly gray-faced and promised me a steak dinner for getting in on time. That's one pledge I'm going to collect....

Love,

Madge

—Source: "Letters, April 7, June 5, December 8, December 22, 1943; April 9, June 2, 1944," by Madge Rutherford by permission of The Woman's Collection, Texas Woman's University.

MARY ANNA MARTIN—CLASS 44-W-10

October 17, 1944

Dearest Folks,

…. We had a very tragic thing happen this morning. One of the girls in 44-W-9 crashed on the long 2,000 mile cross country. It hit some of the girls in her class pretty hard. It seems that we go along so long that accidents never enter our minds. The news of her death so shocked the entire field that our C.O. and one of the staff officers immediately flew over to Memphis, Tenn. to take care of the situation. And they are trying to keep it as secret as possible so that it will not get into the newspapers. We haven't the slightest idea what happened, except that she was off-course and was evidently lost. However, we have had a marvelous record when it comes to fatal accidents, in fact, it is very much higher than the cadet record. But don't you worry about me. I'll always get her down sunny-side-up somehow. I do think I've missed part of flying though if I don't have a forced landing or get lost.

Today I was so thrilled. I got somebody to take my place here at the O.D. [Officer of the Day] office while I went to the flight-line. I took my first cross country. It was just a wee one, but I got a big bang out of it. It was 169 miles long and only took an hour and nine minutes. We really zipped by those check points before I could figure my ground speed. When I finally caught up with the plane we had already reached the destination on one of the legs. We had a tail wind and were averaging 198 mph. But coming back on another leg we bucked the wind and only averaged 140 mph, while airspeed said we were cruising at 160. I know I'm going to like cross-countries. There is just one thing worries me. My instructor did most of the flying today while I read the map, etc. Tomorrow he just goes along for the ride and I pretend I'm solo. How in the world will I be able to fly the airplane at a certain speed and altitude while I have a map in one hand looking for check points, with a computer around my neck to figure ground speed and true heading and write down my ETA and ATA on my knee board. I'll be worn out....

Good night and love,

Mary Anna

—Source: "Letter, October 17, 1944," by Mary Anna Martin by permission of The Woman's Collection, Texas Woman's University.

After graduation from the training program at Sweetwater, some WASP were sent immediately to ferrying assignment; others were given additional specialized training. After receiving instruction on instrument flying on the B-25, Caro Bayley was transferred to Biggs Army Air Field in El Paso, Texas where she piloted bombers pulling tow target sleeves for antiaircraft trainees and flew pursuit planes (fighters).

Graduate Madge Rutherford was first assigned ferrying duties at Long Beach, California. Later she studied instrument flying in St. Joseph, Missouri and at Brownsville Texas Airbase she flew pursuit planes. These excerpts from her letters home demonstrate the aplomb with which these women accepted and coped with the often capricious nature of the aircraft they flew and the sudden emergencies which occurred quite frequently.

CARO BAYLEY—CLASS 43-W-7

Tuesday [Feb. 1944]

Dear Mommie,

…. We work with the anti-aircraft ground troops—they practice combat conditions every day in [the] desert and we do what ever they want us to do to make combat conditions—or somebody comes over and wants to have a look at the camaphlage [sic], or at the fort they've just built, etc. And we fly them where ever they say. The mission usually ends up buzzing (strafing) the troops who all jump into their fox holes and it all makes you feel lucky to be in the sky—even though it is in an AT-11 instead of a 25. Guess it won't be as boring as we thought at first….

Love,

Potatoe

May 16 [1944]

Dear Mommie,

Have had quite a few strafing missions lately. In fact am waiting till 2:30 to get in the ship and straf [sic]. The camaphlage is getting pretty good. At 700 feet you can't see anything but when you go down you can see an enormous camp with tents and trucks. The boys are doing a pretty good job of hiding themselves too, especially after I almost chopped one boy's head off because he had the nerve to walk across the road....

Love,

Potatoe

Aug 26, '44

Dear CGB and Capt,

.... Have just come down from an early morning strafe mission—had to get up at 6:00–T.O. [take off] at 6:30. The other day I had to get up at 5:00 and took off as soon as the dawn came. So today I decided I may as well combine some Sat. pleasure flying along with the strafing. Had a wonderful time slow rolling down from 10,000 and strafing everybody I could find. Apparently something joggled loose in the radio and I had no contact with tower. Made a buzz the runway approach, which is illegal in 3rd AF but O.K. when radio is out. Feel much better—flying is no fun when you merely T.O., fly your mission and land.

Thursday we went out to the firing range to fire the carbine (army gun). Didn't 'specially want to go out but we have to qualify and anyway the range officer kept telling me how much it kicked. I was a little wary(?) after the skeet gun that knocked me off my feet every time I fired. We fired the courses and if I had made one more point I would have been a sharp shooter (and maybe have gotten a medal). Most didn't even qualify—only several made higher out of the 30 that went. They are all looking at me like I was dead eye joe and are trying to get a pilot to release me for combat....

Love,

Potatoe

---

5 Nov 44

Dear CGB and Capt,

Potatoe is now a pursuit pilot—checked out in P-47 four days ago and have never been so excited in my life. [Mary C..] Wilson must be living in a heavenly world. It's a wonderful ship and at cruising settings goes 230, is red lined at something like 500 mph and you're not to put the gear or flaps down above 180. The engine doesn't make much more noise than a sewing machine and it purrs. You can hold the stick with two fingers and it's like pushing a ball bearing around. Kaddy checked out the next day and we're both walking around with a pea shooter idea of life—and feeling that we're way above the rest of the girls that are here....

Love,

Potatoe

—Source: "Letters, February, 1944, May 16, 1944, August 26, 1944, November 5, 1944," by Caro Bayley, by permission of the Woman's Collection, Texas Woman's University.

MADGE RUTHERFORD—CLASS 43-W-4

12/8/43

Dearest Mother & Dad:

…. Here I am 9000 feet over the Chihuahua Mountains on the border of Arizona and Mexico. My C-P [co-pilot] and I are taking turns flying this strawberry crate which is another C-78. We must take it to…Hutchison Kansas for wing modification. As it is we are being very careful with it, considering it a jinx airplane with a vinegary personality. Already this trip we have had the radio go out twice, the gear mechanism once, the flaps likewise. Until you've manually wound the gear down in one of these things you don't know what a sore shoulder is. Nothing dangerous, you understand—just pretty nasty delaying little accidents which increase our trip-time and decrease our sweet temper. I have a very nice co-pilot, or pilot, really. It just happened that I got a check before she did and we are making the best of our misfortune. One bright spot looms on the horizon and that is that we will get to do our own Xmas shopping in Juarez tonight. We are now flying under a thick grey overcast which hangs over the pass and obscures the mountain top. It is very lovely to look at, makes the canyons and mesas look very weird and the rock cliffs have a rose tint. Below the clouds the snow line circles the peaks, as sharply defined as though you had sliced and stretched it there….

Love,

Madge

Motel Inn
Bakersfield, California
[12/22/43]

Are you troubled with dry skin? Does your hair become brittle in the winter wind? Fly a "Maytag (a BT) Messerschmindt" and your troubles are over. OK, the pretty shiny little ship I got today furnished my hair & skin with oil for 6 years cosmetic use. About halfway over the pass she began to spit oil back across the hatch. In ten minutes I couldn't see if it was still daylight outside. Smoke began to ooze up from around the firewall and I began to think about getting out. But the engine instruments showed "all clear" and I decided to do more watchful waiting. About this time some fool came up alongside to fly a little formation. I could barely see the shape of the ship thru the oil and I prayed he would see my trouble and stay far away quick, which he finally did. Ten miles out of Bakersfield, I called in for emergency landing and opened the hatch. There my troubles really began. Oil poured into the cockpit—all over me, my flying suit, leather jacket, Ray-bans, hair, face, oh my goodness! But I got her down, with the firetrucks chasing me down the runways after landing. But nothing happened except I've called 13 beauty shops to get a shampoo. Such is the life of a ferry pilot.

Must eat something now.

Love,

Madge

4/9/44

Dearest Mother & Dad:

…. Yesterday morning we had our first flight in the 78…. A near tragedy occurred while we were warming up for take-off. The instructor accidentally cut the engines. I had to climb out with the fire-bottle and hold it while he restarted them up again. About this time a B-25 pulled in front of us and ran his engine up so tremendously that our ship's tail was well up and it kicked like a Texas roan. I hung onto the wings until the engine was started, then crawled back and grabbed the tail by hand holes to try to hold it down. The prop-wash of the 25 actually lifted me into the air, too. About this time the tower saw our difficulty and called the 25 pilot to cut it out. So he did. But I was limp for hours.

In the afternoon I flew the DC-3, made a take off like a piece of sting, and staggered uncertainly out over the river. In the first place, you are so high off the ground in the cockpit you feel like you're flying the Empire State Building. And in landing you level off about 40 feet too high for you and it's just right for the ship.

I did maneuvers; turns and banks, climbs and glides, etc. I like the way the ship trims up. You just lay her over at 300 and she stays there.

Maybe we'll go up now. I have hopes….

Love,

Madge

Friday
6/2/44

Dear Mother & Dad:

…. My last flight today and I was very tired was mercifully short. I had made one landing and was butting around to take off when a jeep came roaring after me and excited flight instructor pointed out to me that my beautiful 100 octane was pouring out the left gas vent under the wing. One said "Take her off and she'll stop." Another said "Cut Her!" I did just that and got out mighty fast. These learned gentlemen could not imagine why this was happening. Meantime the 100 octane spread a lake about the empennage and so I left them. I'll be anxious to know their decision. P-47's siphon gas but P-40's aren't suppose to.

The beauty of flying a liquid cooled engine is that the coolant heats up so fast on the ground that you have to take off before you have time to reconsider. If you had time, you'd probably never take off the first time. Incidentally our ships have charming names emblazed on their streamlined noses. I flew "The Happy Moron" and the "Mad Russian" this morning.

Time for sleep now.

Love,

Madge

—Source: "Letters, April 7, June 5, December 8, December 22, 1943; April 9, June 2, 1944," by Madge Rutherford by permission of The Woman's Collection, Texas Woman's University.

5

CIVIL RIGHTS SUPPORTERS AT HOME

As the United States waged its war against fascism abroad, certain groups of Americans found themselves in a parallel struggle at home, fighting against racism and the violation of their rights as American citizens. Among these groups were Japanese Americans and African Americans.

Because of widespread fear of spying and sabotage, thousands of people of Japanese descent on the Pacific Coast were indiscriminately relocated to camps in remote areas of the country. Sonoko Iwata, a Japanese woman of American birth, was sent with her three children to Poston Relocation Camp in Arizona, while her Japanese-born husband was confined at Lordsburgh Internment Camp in New Mexico. In an effort to clear her husband of suspicion and reunite their family, Mrs. Iwata addressed an appeal to the U.S. Attorney General. Declaring her gratitude for "the privileges [she had] been able to enjoy and share as a part of democratic America" and affirming the loyalty of her spouse to his adopted country, she explains that the suggestion that her husband could be "dangerous to the security of the United States...is a dishonor we cannot bear to face."

Mary Uyesaka, another Japanese American citizen relocated to the camp at Poston, sent a request to Colonel Oveta Culp Hobby that she hasten acceptance of Japanese Americans into the WAAC. "We, as American citizens, have faith in our country and democracy and believe firmly that our destiny lies here in America.... We would like do our share...by volunteering our services to the WAACs."

African Americans, long denied full American citizenship, nevertheless wished to participate in the struggle for the triumph of democratic ideals. Although their services were sorely needed in war production and in the military, these citizens were denied equality of opportunity. For example, Governor Dixon of Alabama turned away African American workers from a textile plant that was producing cloth for the Defense Department, declaring, "I will not permit the employees of the state to be placed in a position where they must abandon the principle of segregation or lose their jobs."

All branches of the military eventually, though at times reluctantly, accepted African Americans into their ranks but failed to provide the equality of treatment democracy implied. The newly created Women's Army Auxiliary Corps, the first to accept black women, practiced discrimination in the recruiting process and segregation in the service. Lenora Robinson, awaiting her "call to active duty" with the WAACs, showed concern about the treatment she was likely to receive in her letter to President Roosevelt: "I am told because of my pigmentation, I shall now be subjected to new experiences both embarrassing and demoralizing…that when I arrive at my post, I shall be discriminated against,…segregated in barracks, service clubs, and recreation facilities…. Mr. President, as a loyal citizen of the United States, I appeal to you for advice that will help me to serve my country as I want to."

The elimination of segregation in the WAC was representative of the endemic struggle over race in America which paralleled the war for democratic ideals abroad. In a letter to President Harry Truman in 1945, civic leader Thomasina Johnson counseled, "We are sure that you have the moral courage to act in celebrating V-E Day and the Third Anniversary of the Women's Army Corps by abolishing segregation and making it a democratic organization fighting for democracy." Despite their disfranchisement, Japanese Americans and African Americans persisted in their attempts to right the wrongs done to them and, against considerable odds, to make their contributions to democracy.

SONOKO IWATA AND MARY UYESAKA

Two of the thousands of Japanese Americans removed from their west coast homes were Sonoko Iwata and Mary Uyesaka who were relocated to camp Poston, Arizona. Despite this blatant violation of their civil rights, each remained loyal to the United States and the following letters testify to their continued devotion and patriotism. Writing to the United States attorney general, Sonoko Iwata gives reassurances of the loyalty of her husband who is being held in a distant internment camp. Mary Uyesaka seeks to serve the country which has denied her rights as a citizen but whose democratic principles she continues to support.

SONOKO IWATA

Block 42, Building 7-D
Poston, Arizona
July 21, 1942

The Honorable Francis Biddle
United States Attorney General
United States Department of Justice
Washington, District of Columbia

Sir:

I'm taking this means to appeal to you for a reconsideration of the decision against Shigezo Iwata, my husband, who was taken into custody on March 11 from Thermal, California; given a hearing on May 15 at Santa Fe, New Mexico where he was detained; and transferred to Lordsburg, New Mexico on June 19 as an internee of war and now identified as ISN-V5-4J-110-C1 and located at Barrack 4, Camp 3, Company 9, Lordsburg Internment Camp.

I am an American citizen of Japanese descent and I believe in the government of the United States. I'm grateful for the privileges I have been able to enjoy and share as a part of democratic America.

The decision you have recently rendered against Shigezo Iwata, my husband, must have been reached after a careful consideration but I am making this appeal to you in the hope that there might be room for reconsideration.

I solemnly affirm that Shigezo Iwata, my husband, has at all times been loyal to America and has always cooperated with our government, observing all regulations and trying his best to add constructively to the welfare of the nation. In the almost five years of our married life, I have always known him to practice simple honesty. He has been open-hearted, too, though markedly reserved. Our life has been a struggle on a small income but always there was hope and ambition for a higher living and we were slowly but surely attaining it. If Shigezo Iwata is returned to his family, now settled at the Poston War Relocation Camp, I can assure you that he will cooperate and unite in efforts to build up this city of Poston which we know is part of democratic America.

This appeal, I make, not because of our three small children who undoubtedly will receive more adequate care if their father could be with them nor for my own desire of keeping our family together since I know that countless number of homes are being permanently broken because of this conflict, but because I firmly believe Shigezo Iwata, my husband, is a loyal resident and has never been or never will be dangerous to the security of the United States. Moreover, to be considered as such is a dishonor we cannot bear to face.

Whenever your final decision, I shall still have faith in God and in our government but I keep praying that you will be able to give Shigezo Iwata a favorable decision.

Any word from you will be greatly appreciated.

Respectfully yours,

Sonoko U. Iwata
(Mrs. Shigezo Iwata)

—Source: The Historical Society of Pennsylvania (HSP), Shigezo and Sonoko Iwata Papers MSS 53, "Letter from Sonoko Iwata to Attorney General Francis Biddle, July 21, 1942."

MARY UYESAKA

15-1-B
Poston, Arizona
March 17, 1943

Col. Oveta Hobby, Director
WAAC Headquarters
War Department
Washington, D.C.

Dear Madam:

May we take this opportunity to express our appreciation and thanks to you for sending us Lt. Roberta House from the Recruiting Office, Phoenix, Arizona to give us information concerning the WAACs. We loved her very much, but regret deeply that she was not here to recruit enlistment at that time. We realized fully the splendid work the members of the WAAC are doing at the present time and we, too, would like very much to be a part of it.

We, as American citizens, have faith in our country and democracy and believe firmly that our destiny lies here in America. Our brothers and friends have volunteered their services as soldiers in the Army of the United States to fight for their country on the battlefronts-to fight for democracy and all that it stands for and to make this world a better place for everyone to live in. All...who are Americans, regardless of race, creed or color must fight together on the battlefronts and at home to realize all of this in the end.

We would like to do our share towards the war efforts of our country, "behind the men behind the gun on the battlefronts" by volunteering our services to the WAACs.

We are very sincere in our wishes and would appreciate any effort on your part to expedite the enlistment of American Japanese into the WAACs.

Very sincerely yours,

Mary Uyesaka

—Source: "Letter to Col. Oveta Culp Hobby, March 17, 1943" by Mary Uyesaka, 54-49 SPWA 291.2, National Archives at College Park, College Park, Maryland.

MARY MCLEOD BETHUNE

The Second World War brought about increased racial tension between black and white Americans as the former increasingly sought jobs in the defense industries and enlisted in the military. Black workers who did gain employment were often denied adequate housing by white landlords and black soldiers were attacked by white civilians. In a collection of essays, <u>What the Negro Wants</u>, *black writers presented the case for the rights of black Americans. In this particular essay, Mary McLeod Bethune, a New Deal activist for civil rights, analyzes the great American contradiction between the principles of democracy and the white supremacy embedded in its culture.*

.... Throughout America today many people are alarmed and bewildered by the manifestation of this world ferment among the Negro masses. We say we are living in a period of "racial tension." They seem surprised that the Negro should be a part to this world movement. Really all true Americans should not be surprised by this logical climax of American education. For several generations colored Americans have been brought up on the Boston Tea Party and the Declaration of Independence; on the principle of equality of opportunity, the possession of inalienable rights, the integrity and sanctity of the human personality. Along with other good Americans the Negro has been prepared to share his part in the fight against an enemy that threatens all these basic American principles. He is fighting now on land and sea and in the air to beat back these forces of oppression and tyranny and discrimination. Why, then, should we be surprised when at home as well as abroad he fights back against these same forces?

One who would really understand this racial tension which has broken out into actual conflict in riots as in Harlem, Detroit, and Los Angeles, must look to the roots and not be confused by the branches and the leaves. The tension rises out of the growing internal pressure of Negro masses to break through the wall of restriction which restrains them from full American citizenship. This mounting power is met by the unwillingness of white America to allow any appreciable breach in this wall.

The hard core of internal pressure among the Negro masses in the United States today is undoubtedly their resentment over the mistreatment of colored men in the armed forces. The Negro faces restrictions in entering certain branches of the service, resistance to being assigned posts according to his ability, and above all there is the failure of the Army and his government to protect him in the uniform of his Country from actual assault by civilians.

Letters from the men in Army camps have streamed into the homes of their parents and friends everywhere, telling of this mistreatment by officers, military police and civilians, of their difficulties in getting accommodations on trains and busses, of numerous incidents of long, tiresome journeys without meals and other concrete evidences of the failure of their government to protect and provide for its men, even when they are preparing to fight in defense of the principles of that government.

They need no agitation by newspaper accounts or the stimulation of so-called leaders. These things are the intimate experiences of the masses themselves. They know them and feel them intensely and resent them bitterly.

You must add to these deep seated feelings a whole series of repercussions of the unfortunate efforts of Negroes to find a place in war production. The absolute denial of employment in many cases, or employment far below the level of their skills, numerous restrictions in their efforts to get training, resistance of labor unions to the improving and utilization of their skills on the job. Pile on to these their inability to get adequate housing even for those employed in war work; and often where houses are available, they are restricted to segregated units in temporary war housing. At the same time they see around them unlimited opportunities offered to other groups to serve their country in the armed forces, to be employed at well-paying jobs, to get good housing financed by private concerns and FHA funds.

Even those observers who have some understanding of the Negro's desire to break through all these restrictions will charge it to superficial causes, such as the agitation of the Negro press and leaders, or they counsel the Negro to "go slow." It is as though they admit that the patient is sick with fever and diagnosis reveals that he needs twelve grains of quinine, but they decide that because he is a Negro they had better give him only six. They admit that he is hungry and needs to be fed, but because he is a Negro they suggest that a half meal will suffice. This approach, of course, is a historical hang-over. It is a product of the half-hearted and timorous manner in which we have traditionally faced the Negro problem in America.

In order to maintain slavery, it was necessary to isolate black men from every possible manifestation of our culture. It was necessary to teach that they were inferior beings who could not profit from that culture. After the slave was freed, every effort has persisted to maintain "white supremacy" and wall the Negro in from every opportunity to challenge this concocted "supremacy." We said the Negro could not learn and we proved it by restricting his educational opportunities. When he surmounted these obstacles and achieved a measure of training, we said he did not know how to use it and proved it by restricting his employment opportunities. When it was necessary to employ him, we saw to it that he was confined to laborious and poorly-paid jobs. After we had made every effort to guarantee that his economic, social and cultural levels were low, we attributed his status to his race. Therefore, as he moved North and West after Reconstruction and during the Industrial Revolution, we saw to it that he was confined to living in veritable ghettos with covenants that were as hard and resistant as the walls of the ghettos of Warsaw.

We met every effort on his part to break through these barriers with stern resistance that would brook no challenge to our concept of white supremacy. Although we guaranteed him full citizenship under the Constitution and its Amendments, we saw to it that he was largely disfranchised and had little part in our hard won ideal of "the consent of the governed." In the midst of this anachronism, we increasingly educated his children in the American way of life—in its ideals of equality of all men before the law, and opportunities for the fullest possible development of the individual.

As this concept took hold among the Negro masses, it has evidenced itself through the years in a slow, growing, relentless pressure against every restriction which denied them their full citizenship. This pressure, intensified by those of other races who really believed in democracy, began to make a break through the walls here and there. It was given wide-spread impetus by the objectives of the New Deal with its emphasis on the rise of the forgotten man. With the coming of the second World War, all of the Negro's desires were given voice and support by the world leaders who fought back against Hitler and all he symbolizes. His efforts to break out have responded to Ghandi and [Chiang] Kai-Shek, to Churchill and Franklin Roosevelt.

The radios and the press of the world have drummed into his ears the Four Freedoms, which would lead him to think that the world accepts as legitimate his claims as well as those of oppressed peoples all over the world. His drive for status has now swept past even most of his leaders, and has become imbedded in mass-consciousness which is pushing out of the way all the false prophets, be they white or black—or, be they at home or abroad.

The Negro wants to break out into the free realm of democratic citizenship. We can have only one of two responses. Either we must let him out wholly and completely in keeping with our ideals, or we must mimic Hitler and shove him back....

—Source: Draft of essay by Mary McLeod Bethune for <u>What the Negro Wants</u> in the records of the National Council of Negro Women, Series 5, Box 33,

Folder 1, National Park Service—Mary McLeod Bethune Council House NHS, Washington, D.C.

WACs

African American women who chose to aid in the fight for democracy by joining the Women's Army Auxiliary Corps encountered many obstacles because of their color. Some were shunned in the recruitment process; others suffered insults rooted in the military's insidious belief in Negro inferiority. All black WAACs, including officers, were forced to cope with an official position that promoted "separate but equal" treatment but which, in fact, tacitly accepted actions that violated their rights. The following letters highlight the difficulties faced by these women.

MARY ELNORA WHITE

Puzzled and frustrated by the subterfuge of biased WAAC enlistment officers during her three month attempt to enlist, Mary Elnora White seeks help in resolving the situation.

R.F.D. #2
Paducah, Kentucky
July 1, 1943

TO WHOM IT MAY CONCERN:

Sometime ago I wrote you concerning my desire to join the W.A.A.C. and was told to take the matter up with the local W.A.A.C. recruiting officer. I took the letter to the office and was told by the assistant there that the Lieutenant was not in but would be in the next day; I took the letter back the following day and was told by the assistant that the Lieutenant had a sudden and unexpected call to a city and would be gone for three weeks. That was not true at all. They were only trying to dishearten me. I understand from a very reliable source that they have been doing all Negro women that way. I do not understand why they do not want colored women in the W.A.A.C. or don't want to sign them up as a candidate for the W.A.A.C., unless it is because they are prejudiced.

I understand that the organization was for all women irrespective of <u>race color</u> or creed. I was under the impression also that the women appointed to these different towns to induct women were supposed to sign them up on that basis. But these two women do not. They send all colored women on a wild goose chase. Every time they go to the recruiting center, these women have some excuse or put something in their way.

I have gotten tired of being evaded as it were by these women. You do not have your full quota of women in this organization, I understand, and you are eager to get all who are willing. But let me tell you, the reason why you do not have your quota (or the major reason why) is because women like these two are failing to do their duty. They are practicing discrimination and prejudice and these are totally un-American.

Here I am, for instance, ready to offer my very life, the only thing I have to offer, if necessary, in an effort to do my part in this gigantic struggle for the preservation of democracy and the high ideals that we all cherish so highly against totalitarianism and brutality. This is not a White man's war, it is not a black man's war, but it is a war in which all of us must participate, must put all of our efforts, our genius, into, in order to successfully combat the enemy. And it will take both white and colored to do this. You cannot do it by yourselves nor can we. It is a cinch. Together we stand, divided we fall. We are two races within the confines of one country and we must collaborate. Why, the thing that these women here are practicing are the very things the Allies are fighting against, some in the remote corners of the world. Please do something about the existing situation here....

...Notwithstanding all these obstacles I am willing to help and I am sure there is something in the W.A.A.C. I could do. We all have to learn and I would learn to do <u>anything</u> after being in the W.A.A.C. I understand you need women in the Signal Corps. I would learn that or anything. Listen, I have been trying for the past three months or more to join the W.A.A.C. I have been persistent and patient, thinking they would eventually decide to take me, but in vain. You know, there are few women who would volunteer to give their life, if necessary, to sacrifice all their pleasures for this organization. Even if they were, after they found the officials were not wanting their help they wouldn't go the second time. But I have gone the second, third, fourth and innumerable times trying almost begging these women to consider me, but something was always the matter....

Please help me to get into the W.A.A.C. and also help other Negroes farther south.

Yours respectfully,

Mary Elnora White

—Source: "Letter 'To Whom It May Concern,' July 1, 1943" by Mary Elnora White, 54-50-291.2, National Archives at College Park, College Park, Maryland.

LANORA ROBINSON

In Buffalo, New York Lanora Robinson volunteered for the WAAC but she worried about the experience of segregation that awaited her and expressed her concerns in the following letter to President Roosevelt.

198 Laurel Street
Buffalo, New York
December 25, 1942

Mr. Franklin D. Roosevelt
President of the United States
The White House
Washington, D.C.

Dear Sir:

On this anniversary of our Savior's birth, as I await call to active duty in the Women's Army Auxiliary Corps, I find myself questioning my ability to serve to the fullest of my capacity. I am told that because of pigmentation, I shall now be subjected to new experiences both embarrassing and demoralizing.

I hear that when I arrive at my post, I shall be discriminated against, that I shall be segregated in barracks, service clubs, and recreation facilities.

If I am sent to Daytona Beach, Florida, I am told that en route, I shall be "jim-crowed" from the girls of other racial groups who have been friendly and expressed the hope that we will not be separated in our training.

Mr. President, as a loyal citizen of the United States, I appeal to you for advice that will help me to serve my country as I want to. When I am ordered to leave my friends of other racial groups, what as a believer in democratic and christian principles can I say to myself that will give me the will and courage to carry on?

With faith in you and the meaning of Christmas I await your reply.

Most respectfully yours,

LANORA G. ROBINSON

—Source: "Letter to President Franklin D. Roosevelt, December 25, 1942," by Lanora G. Robinson, 55-211-Negro, National Archives at College Park, College Park, Maryland.

CONSTANCE NELSON

Stationed at Camp Forrest, Tennessee, Constance Nelson wrote an open letter to the public about the working conditions for black WACs at her post. The <u>Houston Informer</u> published her letter in May of 1945.

Camp Forrest, Tennessee

Dear People:

> Did not our forefathers fight and die
> For these United States.
> Have we not answered every cry
> To make this nation great?

I am a Negro in Service. I am doing my part for this country. My home is in Chicago, formerly of Texas. I have been in the WAC since WACdom. I am really disheartened more than words can say, that is, I, and thousands of decent girls, abandoned colleges, clubs and friends who were most dear to us to join the Women's Army Corps to do a job and do it well, feeling that we were needed and could do our share to help the boys over there. Upon entering the Women's Army Corps, we were told by WAC officials that we would be given equity, opportunity to exhibit our skill—that is, the qualified ones would have professional jobs, such as dieticians, stenographers, librarians, etc. whereas the less skilled but qualified ones would have the opportunity to go to Army specialist school and complete the course work which was most beneficial. But under no circumstances was it stated that we would be sent to a place like this terrific Camp Forrest, Tenn. and be tossed about like a [ship] on a sandy shore by *white civilians* working on this post.

The only types of jobs here for the educated Negroes (WAC) to do toward victory are: Nurses' Aides (doing all the dirty work), pushing food carts, washing windows, woodwork, scrubbing floors and cooking in the hospital messes, taking orders and being cursed at by civilians working there.

Here if a civilian yells and curses at a WAC and tells her to do something, regardless of what it is, she either executes his orders or is subject to court martial.

Recently a white civilian went to the extreme to strike (slap) a colored WAC and endeavored to pour hot grease on her in one of the messes. And what do you suppose this Tennessee white man got as a punishment? His punishment was a two day lay off with pay and a return to his job at camp. Such drastic occurrences cause more damage than the Japs and Germans together.

Thus I feel that we have made a great sacrifice to join the fight for democracy. We don't want the whites to pity us, but we are true Americans. Our boys are across the sea fighting and dying for this country and the things we all think are worth fighting for, while over here at home and various camps insanity sweeps the South.

I'm sure that all the white people in the South don't approve of such drastic occurrences. It is just the few that are trying to keep America down. America is supposed to be a free country, but without the aid of Negroes it is a doomed country!!!!!

Yours Truly,

Constance E. Nelson, WAC

Please print it all. I didn't have time to type it, but please try to understand my writing. It is vital that the people know about their Colored WACS. Thank you.

—Source: "Letter, May, 1944 by Constance E. Nelson," from We're in This War, Too: Letters from American Women in Uniform, edited by Judy Barrett Litoff and David C. Smith, copyright ¬ 1994 by Judy Barrett Litoff and David C. Smith. Used by permission of Oxford University Press, Inc.

ANONYMOUS

Knowing of her interest in issues of discrimination against blacks, a member of the Army Nurse Corps, stationed at Fort Bragg, North Carolina, writes the following letter to Eleanor Roosevelt requesting her help.

Station Hospital No. 2
Fort Bragg, N.C.
May 3, 1944

Mrs. Franklin D. Roosevelt
The White House
Washington, D.C.

Dear Mrs. Roosevelt,

I am writing you because I have read about the many good things you have done for my race. I hope you will understand, and please help me in any way you can.

We are having trouble with bus transportation here at Fort Bragg, N.C. I was told by the bus driver that he was not allowed to ride colored members of the armed forces on the white busses—that we had to ride only on the colored troop busses. There are approximately eight white busses to one colored bus.

Today I went to my chief nurse's office and reported the situation and asked could anything be done about it. This is the answer I received from the chief nurse, 1st Lt. Evelyn Longmire.

"I guess you will have to WHITEWASH your face."

I told her that I was satisfied with my color and that I do not want to be white. All I am asking for is equal rights....

Why is it we can nurse white soldiers, but when they are well, we cannot ride on the same busses with them? I resigned my position as Public Health Nurse and entered the Army June 1942 to do my patriotic duty. There is so much discrimination here, I have wished a million times I had not entered.

Mrs. Roosevelt, please, help me solve this problem.

—Source: Anonymous "Letter to Mrs. Franklin D. Roosevelt, May 3, 1944," RG 107, Box 25, File 211, National Archives at College Park, College Park, Maryland.

HARRIET WEST

A major in the Women's Army Corps, Harriet West submitted the following report to a War Department office. In it she details the "difficulties" she encountered on an inspection tour of military posts in several southern states.

---

22 February 1944

Subject: Transportation difficulties encountered in the South.
Through: Director, WAC

To: Mr. Truman K. Gibson
Civilian Aide to the Secretary of War
Washington, D.C.

1. In accordance with verbal request from the Civilian Aide to the Secretary of War to the Executive Office of the Director, WAC, the following report is submitted:

    a. On 22 January 1944, the undersigned left Washington, D.C. for Camp Forrest, Tennessee to join Mrs. Lula Garrett Patterson, Women's Editor of the Afro-American newspaper. Other than the necessity for riding in a dirty half-coach from Chattanooga, Tennessee to Tullahoma, Tennessee, no difficulties arose to and from Camp Forrest.

    b. On 25 January 1944, Mrs. Patterson and the undersigned arrived in Anniston, Alabama. Upon leaving the train at Anniston, the undersigned asked the conductor (there being no porter in sight) to lift a regular size suitcase from the train. He remarked, "I don't handle baggage for Niggers." Inasmuch as the trip from Fort McClellan, Alabama (Anniston) to Fort Benning, Georgia was made by private car, no further incident occurred at this point.

    c. On 28 January 1944, Mrs. Patterson and the undersigned drove with two WAC officers from Fort Benning to Columbus, Georgia. Mrs. Patterson and the two WAC officers went into the station to purchase tickets from Columbus to Atlanta. The undersigned went directly to the train to wait for them, standing near the last coach of the train while waiting for the others. A man in workman's clothes, and a cap with a visor approached, saying, "Your coach is down there back of the engine." The undersigned did not answer. He then said, "Hey, you, don't you hear me talking to you." Still no answer. Whereupon he grabbed the undersigned by the arm, turning her around, and called her several *very* vile names, using most *obscene* language, and saying that when Niggers were in that section they respected white people, or words to that effect. The undersigned jerked away saying, "Take your filthy hands away from me, or you won't be able to put them on any other woman," and "Why don't you join the Nazis, that's where you and your kind belong." The man then said he was going to get the police and put the undersigned in jail. He was told to go ahead, whereupon he left going to the station, presumably to get the police. In the meantime, the WAC officers and Mrs. Patterson came out and Mrs. Patterson and the undersigned boarded the train. The coach was filthy, the covers on the seats were black and grimy. So much so, it was necessary to put Kleenex over the seat before sitting down. No further difficulty ensued.

d. On the morning of 29 January 1944, 0925, aboard the Seaboard train #10, Mrs. Patterson and the undersigned asked the porter if it was too late for breakfast. He explained that if we were in the diner within a half an hour we could be served. Upon arriving in the diner we were ushered to a section behind curtains, where four Pullman car porters and two waiters were having breakfast. There were two vacant seats opposite the two waiters. The stewards advised us that that section was for Niggers and that was where we would eat. We refused and returned to our car.

2. It was the understanding of the undersigned that even though separate facilities were provided on trains in the south, they should be equal. It was found that no equal facilities are provided on coaches, on any southern railroad or in the diners on the Seaboard Railroad.

Harriet M. West
Major, WAC

—Source: "Report to Truman K. Gibson, Civilian Aide to the Secretary of War, February 22, 1944," by Major Harriet M. West from We're in This War, Too: Letters from American Women in Uniform, edited by Judy Barrett Litoff and David C. Smith, copyright ¬ 1994 by Judy Barrett Litoff and David C. Smith. Used by permission of Oxford University Press, Inc.

THOMASINA JOHNSON

As the end of the war approached, the U.S. Army remained segregated and black civil rights advocates persisted in their protests. In this letter to President Truman, Thomasina Johnson points out that "separate but equal" is a contradiction in terms and that this form of discrimination inflicts psychological damage not only on those who suffer the injustice but on those who inflict it as well. Three years later, President Truman signed an executive order prescribing equality of treatment and opportunity for service personnel and segregation in the armed forces was officially abolished.

May 8, 1945

Honorable Harry S. Truman
President of the United States of America
The White House
Washington, D.C.

Dear Mr. President:

On Monday, May 14th, the Women's Army Corp will celebrate its Third Anniversary, an anniversary highlighted by V-E Day. We should like to commend the women who make up this section of our armed forces for the highly efficient and exemplary service they have rendered thus far in our total war program and the part they have played in our success. They deserve the admiration of all Americans for their patriotic, unselfish devotion to our country's need. Certainly all American women are proud of the accomplishments of their sisters who wear the khaki.

However, there is a black cloud that hangs over V-E Day and the Third Anniversary of the Women's Army Corp which mars complete satisfaction. That black cloud is segregation. We can think of no more fitting celebration of the Third Anniversary of the Women's Army Corps and V-E Day than that you would issue a directive abolishing segregated Women's Army Corp units of all kinds.

Negro women have served valiantly in this war and deserve to be accorded first-class citizenship without being segregated from all other American women citizens in the Women's Army Corp.

Mr. President, I am sure you realize that there is no such thing as "separate but equal". Mere separation in itself is a form of discrimination. It affects the individual minds of the group against whom it is perpetrated by a sort of indescribable subconscious shame, a stigma. It affects the mind of the perpetrators by a sense of shame, a shame of taking unfair advantage of a group of people whom they outnumber 10-1; by giving the perpetrators a guilt-complex from which they can't escape.

America, whom we all love so dearly, could be the moral leader of the world were it not for race prejudice, discrimination, and segregation. We must rid America of this insidious vice. We are sure that you have the moral courage to act in celebrating V-E Day and the Third Anniversary of the Women's Army Corp by abolishing segregation and making it a democratic organization fighting for democracy.

May we hear from you at your earliest convenience,

Yours very truly,

NATIONAL NON-PARTISAN COUNCIL ON PUBLIC AFFAIRS
OF ALPHA KAPPA ALPHA SORORITY
(Mrs.) Thomasina W. Johnson
Legislative Representative

Copy to: Secretary Stimson
General Marshall
Colonel Hobby

—Source: "Letter of Thomasina W. Johnson to Honorable Harrry S. Truman, May 8, 1945," 54-49-291.2, National Archives at College Park, College Park, Maryland.

6

WAR CORRESPONDENTS

World War II saw the first significant influx of American women war correspondents. Determined not to be restricted to the "safe" areas or the woman's angle, these journalists fought to overcome military resistance and win official accreditation as front line reporters. Early in 1942 they were cleared to cover the European Theater of Operations and many of these women reported from the battlefront, closer to the fighting than women correspondents had ever been before.

Margaret Bourke-White, a photojournalist for <u>Life</u> magazine, accompanied an artillery liaison pilot in his 2-seater Piper Cub as he searched for an enemy installation in Italy's Messerschmitt Alley. While she leaned out of the airplane with her camera, Captain Marinelli radioed in the position of a German gun emplacement and dodged German fighter planes. Later, she photographed the men and the artillery battery who had used Captain Marinelli's calculations to knock out the eight-barreled rocket gun holding back the army's advance near Cassino.

Defying military regulations, <u>Collier's</u> war correspondent, Martha Gellhorn, stowed away on a hospital ship as it crossed the English Channel to Normandy on D-Day Plus One. She learned the stories of the wounded as she helped those who came aboard; at night she joined water ambulance personnel and waded onto the shore to help look for more wounded. Later, in Germany, Gellhorn wrote unsparingly of the horrors at the Dachau concentration camp and was at the camp the day Germany surrendered to the Allies. Gellhorn wrote: "For surely this war was made to abolish Dachau and all the other places like Dachau, and everything that Dachau stood for, and to abolish it forever."

It was not until February of 1945 that women journalists were permitted in the Pacific combat zone where they reported from Navy hospital ships picking up the wounded. Until that time, Admiral Chester Nimitz and General Douglas MacArthur, Commanders in the Pacific, had limited the pool of reporters to men.

Patricia Lochridge, assigned to the Pacific area by the editors of <u>Woman's Home Companion</u>, reported on the prolonged battle for the island of Iwo Jima. Assigned to a hospital ship, she tells individual stories of the wounded including that of one soldier who helped raise the flag on Mt. Suribachi. But she also tells the collective story of Iwo Jima, "…the story of thousands of Marines who fought the toughest, bloodiest battle in their history to give us a stepping stone to Tokyo."

MARGARET BOURKE-WHITE

The most celebrated woman photographer of the 20th century, Margaret Bourke-White, was already known for her dramatic compositions before World War II began. She had been one of <u>Fortune's</u> first photographers and pioneered the photo essay in the early issues of <u>Life</u> magazine.

As the first accredited woman war correspondent of the decade, she worked simultaneously as an Army Air Force photographer for the Pentagon and as a photojournalist for Life. Under orders from General Jimmy Doolittle she became, in January of 1943, the first woman to go on a bombing mission. Later that year, she would take aerial photographs of the Italian Campaign from an unarmed two-seater Piper Cub. She covered the violent ground war in Italy as well, vividly documenting for Life's readers the physical facts of war as American soldiers experienced it, a world of foxholes, land mines, and gunfire. In the second article included here, Bourke-White immerses the reader in this world.

From "Over The Lines"

"This strip is really a nerve jerker," Lieutenant Mike Strok called to me over his shoulder.

We were circling above the tiniest airfield I had ever seen. The landing strip was so pocked with shell craters that I did not see how my Grasshopper pilot was going to slip in among them. It was nothing more than the beaten edge of a plowed field, but for the Air OP's, the "Eyes of the Artillery" as they are called in heavy-gun circles, this strip was their most forward operating base.

Lieutenant Strok had to divide his attention between the shell pits below and the sky above. This was because we were landing in the region airmen called Messerschmitt Alley. If an unarmed, unarmored observation plane such as our Cub is attacked, the pilot's means of escape is to outmaneuver the enemy.

"Good idea to make sure there's no Jerry fighter hanging about," said Lieutenant Strok. "If you can see him first, then he doesn't get the chance to blast the daylights out of you."

A final inspection confirmed that the sky was clear, and he brought our tiny Cub to a standstill on a piece of earth as big as a back yard in Brooklyn.

The commanding officer of the field and his ground crew of one ran up to greet us.

The ground crew spoke first. "If that ain't an American girl, then I'm seeing things!" he exclaimed.

The young officer laughed. "Sorry we're out of red carpet," he said. "We live like gypsies up here."

The CO of the Grasshoppers was twenty-six-year-old Captain Jack Marinelli of Ottumwa, Iowa. He was chief pilot and supervisor for a group of artillery liaison pilots who hedgehopped along the front lines in their Cubs, acting as flying observation posts to spot enemy targets and adjust fire for Fifth Army artillery. I had seldom seen a flier who bore less resemblance to Hollywood's idea of a pilot than Captain Marinelli. He looked more like the tractor and hay-machine demonstrator which I learned he had been back in Iowa before the war. He was plump, pleasant, and easygoing. This last characteristic, I was to find, faded as soon as the enemy was in sight. He had the reputation of being the coolest and most resourceful artillery pilot on the Fifth Army front.

Mike Strok explained that I wanted to take airplane pictures of the front, and Captain Marinelli said, "Well, I've just had a call to go out on a mission. There's a *Nebelwerfer* holding up an infantry division and they asked me to go out and try to spot it. She can come along if she wants to."

"Jees, you don't want to take a girl on a mission," said the ground crew of one.

"She'll go if you'll take her," stated Lieutenant Strok.

"What's a *Nebelwerfer*?" I inquired.

"You've heard of a screaming meemie, haven't you? Wicked weapon! It's a multiple mortar: eight-barreled rocket gun."

By the time the screaming meemie was explained to me, I had been strapped into the observer's seat, and the ground crew was adjusting a parachute to my back and shoulders.

Knowing that one of the functions of observer is to watch all quadrants of the sky for enemy planes, I said to the Captain, "I'm not going to make a very good observer for you. Most of the time I'll have my face buried in my camera, and even when I haven't, I'm not sure I'll know the difference between an enemy fighter and one of ours."

"Don't worry about that," Captain Marinelli said. "If you see anything that looks like an airplane, you tell me and I'll decide whether it's a bandit or an angel."

I placed my airplane camera on my knees and arranged additional equipment and a couple of spare cameras, telephoto lenses, and some aerial filters on the low shelf behind my shoulders. The space was so cramped, and any extra movement so pinched, with the parachute crowded on my back, that I wanted to be sure I had everything near at hand where I could reach it in a hurry. There was no room in the Cub to wear helmets, as our heads touched the roof. Someone had lent me one of the fur caps used by our Alaska troops, and I tucked my hair back under it and tied it firmly around my chin. When you lean out into the slipstream with an airplane camera, any escaping strand of hair will lash into your eyes and sometimes blind you during just that vital second when you are trying to catch a picture. The Captain lowered the whole right side of the airplane, folding it completely out of the way so I would have an unobstructed area in which to lean out and work. Then he spoke into his microphone. "Mike-Uncle-Charlie! This is Mike-Uncle-Charlie five-zero. I'm taking off on a mission. Stand by!"

"Who is Mike-Uncle-Charlie?" I asked.

"That's our brigade HQ's code word for today," replied the Captain. "Just our phonetic alphabet for MUC—today's call letters. When I find something that radio guy will be sitting up there with his ear phones on, listening."

The ground crew spun the props. "We'll be back in time for lunch," shouted Captain Marinelli to Lieutenant Strok as we started to taxi between the shell craters. I glanced at my watch, which registered quarter after eleven, and couldn't help wondering if we really would be back for lunch. I was trying hard not to wonder whether we would be back at all....

◆ ◆ ◆

An instant later we were flying over a desolate stretch of road with no traffic at all. This, then, was no man's land. At the farther end we saw a beautifully arched ancient bridge, its masonry quite intact.

"Jerry territory," said the Captain, and took the plane sharply upward.

Over our own side the Cubs make a practice of flying low, because this makes an attack by enemy fighters more difficult, as they cannot come in under; but when the observation planes cross the lines, they must increase altitude, for without armor they are very vulnerable to small-arms fire.

In search of the German rocket gun, we flew four miles over enemy territory and Captain Marinelli began hunting for the *Nebelwerfer* in the region of San Angelo.

"That's the 'Gargling River,'" he pointed out. "GI for Garigliano. And there's the Rapido." The road to Rome stretched forward into the distance, with a railroad running parallel some distance to the left. A hairpin turn branched upward toward the Benedictine monastery, at that time still intact. The ruins of Cassino lay in white smudges at the foot of snowcapped Mt. Cairo.

Cassino corridor presented an extraordinary appearance, with white plumes rising up at intervals from the valley floor. These were phosphorus shells from our own Long Toms, falling on the enemy. Whenever one landed close below us we could see it opening out into a pointed splash of fire, which quickly became transformed into a rising chunk of smoke....

Just then he picked up the flash of the German *Nebelwerfer*—too quick for my untrained eye—and caught sight of the shrubbery blowing back on the ground from the gun blast.

"Mike-Uncle-Charlie," he spoke into his microphone. "This is Mike-Uncle-Charlie five-zero. Enemy gun battery located at co-ordinate 86-16-2. I can observe. Over."

Then to me, over his shoulder, "It's going to take them a little time now, because they've got to compute their data and consult their fire-direction chart to see which guns can reach the target. They'll let me know when they've assigned a battery. We'll be hanging right around here, so speak up if you want to be put into position for anything special."

There were many things that I wanted to be put into position for. Below us it looked as though someone were shaking an enormous popcorn shaker with white grains of popcorn bursting all over the valley floor. These were thickest in front of Cassino. The Captain maneuvered the plane so that I was practically lying on my side over the valley, and—strapped in safely—I could get an unobstructed view of the battleground below.

In a few minutes a message came through that Xray-King-Item would fire. While I took pictures of the popcorn-sprinkled valley, Marinelli carried on his radio conversation with Xray-King-Item, the battery assigned to knock out the *Nebelwerfer*.

I was overwhelmed to learn that it would be my pilot, up in our little Cub, who would actually give the command to fire. The next message he received was, "Mike-Uncle-Charlie five-zero, this is Xray-King-Item. Will fire on your command. Over."

"Fire," said Marinelli, and the reply came back, "Seventy-two seconds. On the way."....

On the seventy-second second, a white geyser began rising toward us from below, and we knew that this was Xray-King-Item's smoke shell. Marinelli spoke into his microphone: "Xray-King-Item; this is Mike-Uncle-Charlie five zero; five hundred yards right, one hundred yards short. Over."

Then he explained, "We've got to give them a little time again to make their correction. They're laying number-one gun on it now. When they get it adjusted they'll tie in the whole battery."

Soon another message came from Xray-King-Item: seventy-two seconds on the way. Again at the end of seventy-two seconds a feather of smoke rose from below. The aim was closer now: "Five-zero right; seven-zero short," Captain Marinelli radioed.

I realized that the Captain was handling a great many tasks at once. Not only was he checking his watch during each seventy-two-second interval, radioing his sensings in terms of deflection and elevation data, but he was keeping an eye on the sky for enemy planes. And taking care of me, too! Every time I saw a fresh shell burst I would yell to be put in position, and he would maneuver the Cub so I could photograph while he observed.

Suddenly he exclaimed, "We're being shot at." We could hear faint sounds as though twigs were snapping against the plane—a little like hot grease spitting in a frying pan just beyond us. "It's a Spandau," said Marinelli, and he knew exactly what to do. Since the Spandau, a German machine gun, has an effective range up to 2400 feet, he simply circled up to 3200 feet, where he went on making his observations and I went on taking photographs.

"Hands cold?" he called.

They were almost numb. At our higher altitude the air was colder and I had been leaning out into the windstream with the camera. The Captain, more protected by the nose of the Cub, stripped off his gloves and gave them to me.

The whole process of adjusting fire had gone on for about fourteen minutes when Captain Marinelli finally radioed, "Deflection correct, range correct, Fire for effect."

"They're bringing in several batteries this time," said the Captain. "And this time it will be HE shells."

At the end of seventy-two seconds we could see that whole area being blanketed, not with white smoke bursts as before, but with the deadlier high-explosive shells. Curls and twists of black smoke spurted over the ground and billowed upward, and we knew that the *Nebelwerfer* was being chewed to bits.

"This is Mike-Uncle-Charlie five-zero," called Captain Marinelli. "Target area completely covered. Fire effective. Enemy battery neutralized."

Less than a minute later he exclaimed, "I see a fighter." Then, "I see two fighters."

Coming around Mt. Cevaro I could see them too: a black speck growing larger and behind it another smaller speck. In less time than it takes to tell, they had taken on the size and shape of airplanes.

We were in such a steep dive by that time that I was practically standing on my head, when I heard Marinelli say, "I see four fighters."

Sure enough, there were four shapes coming toward us, looking unmistakably like Focke-Wulf 190's.

This was the steepest dive I had ever been in in my life. I tried to take a picture, a plan I very quickly had to abandon because, with the whole side of the plane completely open, and the shelf behind me full of cameras and lenses, it was all I could do to hold back my equipment with my elbows and shoulders, to keep it from sailing into space.

I was bracing myself with the back of my neck when Captain Marinelli exclaimed, "I've lost my mike. Can you find my mike for me?" I knew he needed his microphone so he could report the fighters as a warning to all the other Cubs in the air. Groping with my left hand, and holding back my cameras with my right elbow, I retrieved his mike and handed it to him. We were still gliding down at a terrific angle when he reported, "Four enemy fighters sighted."

We were within fifteen feet of the ground when he pulled out of that dive. I have never seen such flying. He ducked into a gully and began snaking along a stream bed. Soon we were behind a small hill and over our own territory, where the fighters could not follow us in so low. In another instant we were behind a mountain and blocked from sight of the enemy planes.

We flew back to our field in time for mess, and when we rolled into the tiny landing strip, the ground crew came running up, bursting with news. To Captain Marinelli this news was much more exciting than being chased by four Focke-Wulfs: there was steak for lunch.

From "155-mm. Flash Bulb"

Even in the daytime the battery CP was always in a half twilight. It had been dug deep in the earth and was lighted by candles melted onto distinctive holders—jagged pieces of shrapnel. These were not just any flak fragments. Each piece, I was to learn, was one to which some crew member had a personal attachment because it had missed him.

When I crawled down into the dugout, the gun computer, a young lad who had grown an amazing mustache, looked up from his chart, his eyes popping.

"Jees," he exclaimed. "We'd heard that a lady had been seen taking pictures from foxholes, but we didn't believe it. Do my eyes deceive me?"

"Wake up," said another boy. "This is *Life* goes to a party with Long Toms. Isn't that the idea?" he asked, turning to me.

"Something like that," I replied. "I thought it might be nice to be at the sending end of artillery instead of the receiving end for a change."

"We can't guarantee that you'll see only the sending end of things tonight," they explained. "We never can tell when we'll get counterbattery."

Counterbattery is a matter of answering back at the enemy. Whenever you can spot his gun position you aim at his battery and try to wash him out. He does the same to you. Counterbattery is a game that both sides can play.

"We've been under a lucky star lately," said the battery executive. "It's a month since we've written any names on shells."

"What do you mean, writing names on shells?" I inquired.

"We have a custom in our battalion," the battery executive explained. "When the Krauts fire counterbattery, and we lose any men, we write the names of the men we have lost on the very next shell we fire."...

...It was beginning to grow dark, and time to load up cameras and guns. I had planned to work all night with the heavy artillery, because I wanted to learn what a night in the life of a gun crew was like.

"Hope you don't have an artillery duel," said the mess sergeant as we started out of the cellar. "Hope you're quick at getting into foxholes," wished the KP, "or you'll get dents in your helmet."

When we reached Number 2 gun in Abel battery, the first thing the Lieutenant did was to show me the nearest foxhole, in case I should need it in a hurry, and then I was introduced to the gun crew.

I had seldom seen people more thrilled about having their pictures taken. It seemed to them too good to be true that their own battery, for which they had an almost human affection, had been selected for photographs. They had worked with these 155's throughout the whole Italian campaign, and had named their battery Superman.

"How'd you come to pick our battery?" they asked. Usually these choices are the result of chance, but this time there had been a reason. It had been the idea of the Grasshopper pilots, who had been flying me from spot to spot during my work at the Italian front, to arrange for me to photograph the same battery whose smoke puffs I had caught in my pictures over Cassino valley. This was the battery with which Captain Marinelli had been in communication the day I had flown his mission with him, and it was these very Long Toms which had knocked out the German *Nebelwerfer*. Although Superman had moved periodically forward every time our troops had made an appreciable advance, Captain Marinelli was still air-liaison officer for the battalion.

As I ran around getting cameras ready, the boys warned me that there were two types of stakes I should stay away from. The first were aiming stakes, which the guns were "laid on" to put them on the "base point." The others were sticks marking small disturbed areas of ground.

"What's in there?" I asked.

"We don't know exactly," I was told. "Possibly mines. But we don't like the looks of those spots, and there's been no chance yet to investigate. Healthier just to keep away."

The crew pushed back the camouflage net from the muzzle of the Long Tom. The heavy barrel, which had been depressed out of sight under the net, rose majestically into firing position. Squatting on the edge of the gulch, camouflage still blanketing its flanks, the great gun looked like some oversized mechanical giraffe sitting on its haunches, stretching out its long neck to survey the landscape.

The moon rose from behind a translucent rim of misty hills, and a thin line of silver slid along the gun tube like a sword. A red light drifted up above us; it was a lighted meteorological balloon. By following it with an instrument that measured its speed as it moved, it was possible to apply weather corrections on the flight of shells.

It seemed mysterious and extraordinary to me that a streamlined missile like a shell, making a journey faster than sound, could be blown off its course by the wind. But I had been told that in the projectile's fourteen-mile journey, even the earth's rotation would have time to affect its aim. Already the Abel computer whom I had seen in the Fire Direction Center had allowed for the world to turn fifty yards under the shell's swift path.

The crew helped me plot out camera positions. Each time the gun fired I wanted to get four different effects with four different cameras. It was hard to judge with the eye how far into space the flash from the gun extended, or how much photographic light it gave out. I was particularly eager to get one picture from as far toward the front as practical, to get the fullest possible effect of the muzzle flash. The men helped me choose a position where I would not be blown off my feet by the concussion, and they helped me ease into it gradually, trying it a little farther with each round until we had achieved the desired viewpoint. They gave me cotton for my ears so that I would not be deafened by the blast.

Each time the gun fired, the whole crew turned away from the flash and shut their eyes tight, and at the same time put their fingers in their ears and opened their mouths wide to protect their eardrums from the concussion. Getting the faces of the gun crew in action was an important picture in the series; Padgitt [her assistant assigned by the Army] could be trusted to catch this as he had a quick trigger finger. I set his camera with one midget flash bulb to throw a slight illumination on the men's faces. The other two cameras I placed to catch other viewpoints, and the force of relief gunners divided into two groups to man each camera.

The crew chief called out his commands: *Load! Ready!! Fire!!!* The great gun let forth a roar, and each of us from our various locations tried to catch it at the exact instant of firing. Then I ran from my post at the side-forward angle of the gun, watching where I ran in the moonlight so as not to trip over the mine stakes, and changed the films and reset the cameras for the next round. Since there were several minutes between rounds, I had time to figure out new viewpoints, take measurements, and reset the focus between each firing of the gun.

There was so much interest in photography that night that relief crews from Baker and Charlie batteries came up to help during the hours they were off duty. Soon practically everyone not actually engaged in loading and firing a Long Tom was busy holding film packs, moving tripods, handling lens hoods and camera gadgets, helping me get the four cameras set up and synchronized in time for each round from the gun.

In order to catch each picture at the exact second of firing such close timing was needed, and we had so many signals to one another, that finally the boys said: "We think it would be easier if you would give the command to fire."

It isn't very often that a war correspondent gets the chance to command a Long Tom firing at a bridge by Cassino, and I was delighted. So each time the next round was due, I would yell *load—ready—fire* at the top of my lungs, and four pictures would be taken on four cameras while that 155-mm. shell crashed into space.

It was a little after midnight when the Brigadier General of the artillery brigade came along. He had heard that some pictures were being taken, and he dropped by to see what was going on. Everybody was so busy by that time, synchronizing the shooting of cameras with the firing of guns, that no one stopped for formalities with the Brigadier General.

So many camera gadgets were being passed from one man to another that soon the BG found his hands full of film-pack adapters, cable releases, and film slides. By that time the enthusiasm for photography had risen to such a pitch that it wasn't much longer before the General was operating my camera while I was giving the command to fire.

—Source: <u>They Call It 'Purple Heart Valley'</u> by Margaret Bourke-White, published by Simon and Schuster, 1944, 1969. Reprinted by permission of the Margaret Bourke-White Estate and its agent, Barry N. Malzberg.

MARTHA GELLHORN

Another major magazine at the time was <u>Collier's</u>, whose editors had previously hired Martha Gellhorn to cover the Spanish Civil War (1936–1939). The magazine called upon the experience Gellhorn had gained reporting on that conflict and assigned her to observe and describe events of World War II for their readers. In extended essays, Gellhorn helped readers visualize two of the war's major events, the Normandy Invasion and the liberation of Nazi concentration camps.

D-Day, June 6, 1944, saw three million Allied soldiers, 9,000 ships and landing craft, and 11,000 airplanes move across the English Channel to France. From her vantage point on a hospital ship, Gellhorn described the vast armada and told the story of the wounded soldiers evacuated from the beaches.

On a subsequent assignment, Gellhorn was a witness to the Holocaust. The Nazis, over a period of ten years, had exterminated seven to eight million prisoners, six million of them Jews. Many were killed in gas chambers, others through medical experiments, hard labor, torture and starvation. Several days after the liberation of the concentration camp at Dachau, Gellhorn gave her readers an unsparing tour of the routine horrors inflicted there in language so detailed and graphic as to preclude forgetting.

from "The First Hospital Ship"

There were four hundred and twenty-two bunks covered with new blankets, and a bright, clean well-equipped operating room, never before used. Great cans marked "Whole Blood" stood on the decks. Plasma bottles and supplies of drugs and bales of bandages were stored in handy places. Everything was ready and any moment the big empty hospital ship would be leaving for France.

The ship itself was painfully white. The endless varied ships clotted in this English invasion port were gray or camouflaged and they seemed to have the right idea. We, on the other hand, were all fixed up like a sitting pigeon. Our ship was snowy white with a green line running along the sides below the deck rail, and with many bright new red crosses painted on the hull and painted flat on the boat deck. We were to travel alone, and there was not so much as a pistol on board in the way of armament, and neither the English crew and ship's officers nor the American medical personnel had any notion of what happened to large conspicuous white ships when they appeared at a war, though everyone knew the Geneva agreement concerning such ships and everyone wistfully hoped that the Germans would take the said agreement seriously.

There were six nurses aboard. They came from Texas and Michigan and California and Wisconsin, and three weeks ago they were in the U.S.A. completing their training for this overseas assignment. They had been prepared to work on a hospital train, which would mean caring for wounded in sensible, steady railway carriages that move slowly through the green English countryside. Instead of which they found themselves on a ship, and they were about to move across the dark, cold green water of the Channel. This sudden switch in plans was simply part of the day's work and each one, in her own way, got through the grim business of waiting for the unknown to start, as elegantly as she could. It was very elegant indeed, especially if you remembered that no one aboard had ever been on a hospital ship before, so the helpful voice of experience was lacking.

We had pulled out of the harbor in the night, but we crossed by daylight and the morning seemed longer than other mornings. The captain never left the bridge and, all alone and beautifully white, we made our way through a mine-swept lane in the Channel. The only piece of news we had, so far, was that the two hospital ships which preceded us struck mines on their way over, fortunately before they were loaded with wounded soldiers and without serious damage to the personnel aboard. Everyone silently hoped that three would be a lucky number; and we waited very hard; and there was nothing much to see except occasional ships passing at a distance.

Then we saw the coast of France and suddenly we were in the midst of the armada of the invasion. People will be writing about this sight for a hundred years and whoever saw it will never forget it. First it seemed incredible; there could not be so many ships in the world. Then it seemed incredible as a feat of planning; if there were so many ships, what genius it required to get them here, what amazing and unimaginable genius. After the first shock of wonder and admiration, one began to look around and see separate details. There were destroyers and battleships and transports, a floating city of huge vessels anchored before the green cliffs of Normandy. Occasionally you would see a gun flash or perhaps only hear a distant roar, as naval guns fired far over those hills. Small craft beetled around in a curiously jolly way. It looked like a lot of fun to race from shore to ships in snub-nosed boats beating up the spray. It was no fun at all, considering the mines and obstacles that remained in the water, the sunken tanks with only their radio antennae showing above water, the drowned bodies that still floated past. On an LCT near us washing was hung up on a line, and between the loud explosions of mines being detonated on the beach dance music could be heard coming from its radio. Barrage balloons, always looking like comic toy elephants, bounced in the high wind above the massed ships, and invisible planes droned behind the gray ceiling of cloud. Troops were unloading from big ships to heavy cement barges or to light craft, and on the shore, moving up four brown roads that scarred the hillside, our tanks clanked slowly and steadily forward.

Then we stopped noticing the invasion, the ships, the ominous beach, because the first wounded had arrived. An LCT drew alongside our ship, pitching in the waves; a soldier in a steel helmet shouted up to the crew at the aft rail, and a wooden box looking like a lidless coffin was lowered on a pulley, and with the greatest difficulty, bracing themselves against the movement of their boat, the men on the LCT laid a stretcher inside the box. The box was raised to our deck and out of it was lifted a man who was closer to being a boy than a man, dead white and seemingly dying. The first wounded man to be brought to that ship for safety and care was a German prisoner.

Everything happened at once. We had six water ambulances, light motor launches, which swung down from the ship's side and could be raised the same way when full of wounded. They carried six litter cases apiece or as many walking wounded as could be crowded into them. Now they were being lowered, with shouted orders: "That beach over there where they've got two red streamers up." "Just this side of Easy Red." We lay at anchor halfway between those now famous and unhealthy beaches, Easy Red and Dog Red. "Take her in slow." "Those double round things that look like flat spools are mines." "You won't clear any submerged tanks so look sharp." "Ready?" "Lower her!"

The captain came down from the bridge to watch this. He was feeling cheerful, and he now remarked, "I got us in all right but God knows how we'll ever get out." He gestured toward the ships that were as thick around us as cars in a parking lot. "Worry about that some other time."

The stretcher-bearers, who were part of the American medical personnel, started on their long back-breaking job. By the end of that trip their hands were padded with blisters and they were practically hospital cases themselves. For the wounded had to be carried from the shore into our own water ambulances or into other craft, raised over the side, and then transported down the winding stairs of this converted pleasure ship to the wards. The ship's crew became volunteer stretcher-bearers instantly. Wounded were pouring in now, hauled up in the lidless coffin or swung aboard in the motor ambulances; and finally an LST tied alongside and made itself into a sort of landing jetty, higher than the light craft that ran the wounded to us, but not as high as our deck. So the wounded were lifted by men standing on the LST, who raised the stretchers high above their heads and handed them up to men on our deck, who caught hold of the stretcher handles. It was a fast, terrifying bucket-brigade system, but it worked.

Belowstairs all partitions had been torn out and for three decks the inside of the ship was a vast ward with double tiers of bunks. The routine inside the ship ran marvelously, though four doctors, six nurses and about fourteen medical orderlies were very few people to care for four hundred wounded men. From two o'clock one afternoon until the ship docked in England again the next evening at seven, none of the medical personnel stopped work. And besides plasma and blood transfusions, re-dressing of wounds, examinations, administering of sedatives or opiates or oxygen and all the rest, operations were performed all night long. Only one soldier died on that ship and he had come aboard as a hopeless case.

It will be hard to tell you of the wounded, there were so many of them. There was no time to talk; there was too much else to do. They had to be fed, as most of them had not eaten for two days; shoes and clothing had to be cut off; they wanted water; the nurses and orderlies, working like demons, had to be found and called quickly to a bunk where a man suddenly and desperately needed attention; plasma bottles must be watched; cigarettes had to be lighted and held for those who could not use their hands; it seemed to take hours to pour hot coffee, via the spout of a teapot, into a mouth that just showed through bandages.

But the wounded talked among themselves and as time went on we got to know them, by their faces and their wounds, not their names. They were a magnificent enduring bunch of men. Men smiled who were in such pain that all they really can have wanted to do was turn their heads away and cry, and men made jokes when they needed their strength just to survive. And all of them looked after each other, saying, "Give that boy a drink of water," or "Miss, see that Ranger over there, he's in bad shape, could you go to him?" All through the ship men were asking after other men by name, anxiously, wondering if they were on board and how they were doing....

When night came, the water ambulances were still churning in to the beach looking for wounded. Someone on an LCT had shouted out that there were maybe a hundred scattered along there somewhere. It was essential to try to get them aboard before the nightly air raid and before the dangerous dark cold could eat into their hurt bodies. Going in to shore, unable to see, and not knowing this tricky strip of water, was slow work. Two of the launch crew, armed with boat hooks, hung over the side of the boat and stared at the black water, looking for obstacles, sunken vehicles, mines, and kept the hooks ready to push us off the sand as we came closer in. For the tides were a nasty business too, and part of the time wounded had to be ferried out to the water ambulances on men's shoulders, and part of the time the water ambulances simply grounded and stuck on the beach together with other craft, stranded by the fast-moving sea.

We finally got onto a cement troop barge near the beach called Easy Red. The water ambulance could not come inshore near enough to be of any use at this point, so it left us to look for a likelier anchorage farther down. We waded ashore in water to our waists, having agreed that we would assemble the wounded from this area on board a beached LST and wait until the tide allowed the water ambulance to come back and call for us. It was almost dark by now and there was a terrible feeling of working against time.

Everyone was violently busy on that crowded dangerous shore. The pebbles were the size of melons and we stumbled up a road that a huge road shovel was scooping out. We walked with the utmost care between the narrowly placed white tape lines that marked the mine-cleared path, and headed for a tent marked with a Red Cross just behind the beach. Ducks [amphibious jeeps] and tanks and trucks were moving down this narrow rocky road and one stepped just a little out of their way, but not beyond the tapes. The dust that rose in the gray night light seemed like the fog of war itself. Then we got off on the grass and it was perhaps the most surprising of all the day's surprises to smell the sweet smell of summer grass, a smell of cattle and peace and the sun that had warmed the earth some other time when summer was real.

Inside the Red Cross tent two tired unshaven dirty polite young men said that the trucks were coming in here with the wounded and where did we want to have them unloaded? We explained the problem of the tides and said the best thing was to run the trucks down to that LST there and carry the wounded aboard, under the canvas roof covering, and we would get them off as soon as anything floated. At this point a truck jolted up and the driver shouted out a question and was told to back and turn. He did not need to be told to do this carefully and not get off the mine-cleared area. The Red Cross men said they didn't know whether wounded would be coming in all night or not—it was pretty tough to transport them by road in the dark; anyway they'd send everything down to our agreed meeting place and everyone said, well good luck fella, and we left. No one wasted time talking around there. You had a feeling of fierce and driven activity, with the night only being harder to work in than the day.

We returned to our small unattractive stretch of the beach and directed the unloading of this truck. The tide was coming in and there was a narrow strip of water between the landing ramp of the LST and the shore. The wounded were carried carefully and laid on the deck inside the great whale's-mouth cavern of the LST. After that there was a pause, with nothing to do. Some American soldiers came up and began to talk. This had been an ugly piece of beach from the beginning and they were still here, living in foxholes and supervising the unloading of supplies. They spoke of snipers in the hills a hundred yards or so behind the beach, and no one lighted a cigarette. They spoke of not having slept at all, but they seemed pleased by the discovery that you could go without sleep and food and still function all right. Everyone agreed that the beach was a stinker and it would be a great pleasure to get the hell out of here sometime. Then there was the usual inevitable comic American conversation: "Where're you from?" This always fascinates me; there is no moment when an American does not have time to look for someone who knows his home town. We talked about Pittsburgh and Rosemont, Pa. and Chicago and Cheyenne, not saying much except that they were sure swell places and a damn sight better than this beach. One of the soldiers remarked that they had a nice little foxhole about fifty yards inland and we were very welcome there when the air raid started if we didn't mind eating sand, which was unavoidable in their nice little foxhole.

A stretcher-bearer from the hospital ship thanked them for their kind invitation and said that on the other hand we had guests aboard the LST and we would have to stay home this evening. I wish I had ever known his name because I would like to write it down here. He was one of the best and jolliest boys I've met any place, any time. He joked no matter what happened, and toward the end of that night we really began to enjoy ourselves. There is a point where you feel yourself so small and helpless in such an enormous insane nightmare of a world, that you cease to give a hoot about anything and you renounce care and start laughing.

He went off to search for the water ambulances and returned to say there wasn't a sign of them, which meant they couldn't get inshore yet and we'd just have to wait and hope they could find this spot when it was black night. If they never found this place the LST would float later, and the British captain said he would run our wounded out to the hospital ship, though it would not be for hours. Suddenly our flak started going up at the far end of the beach and it was beautiful, twinkling as it burst in the sky, and the tracers were as lovely as they always are—and no one took pleasure from the beauty of the scene. "We've had it now," said the stretcher-bearer. "There isn't any place we can put those wounded." I asked one of the soldiers, just for interest's sake, what they did in case of air raids and he said, well, you could go to a foxhole if you had time, but on the other hand there wasn't really much to do. So we stood and watched and there was altogether too much flak for comfort. We could not hear the planes nor hear any bomb explosions but as everyone knows flak is a bad thing to have fall on your head.

The soldiers now drifted off on their own business and we boarded the LST to keep the wounded company. It seemed a specially grim note to be wounded in action and then have to lie helpless under a strip of canvas while any amount of steel fragments, to say nothing of bombs, could drop on you and complete the job. The stretcher-bearer and I said to each other gloomily that as an air-raid shelter far better things than the hold of an LST had been devised, and we went inside, not liking any of it and feeling miserably worried about our wounded....

The night, like the morning, went on longer than other nights. Our water ambulances found us, and there was a lot of good incomprehensible Cockney talk among the boatmen while the wounded were loaded from the now floating LST to the small, bucking launch. We set out, happy because we were off the beach and because the wounded would be taken where they belonged. The trip across that obstacle-studded piece of water was a chatty affair, due to the boat crew. "Crikey, mate, wot yer trying ter do, ram a destroyer?" And "By God, man, keep an eye in yer head for God's sake that's a tank radio pole." To which another answered, "Expect me to see a bloody piece of grass in this dark?" So, full of conversation, we zigzagged back to the hospital ship and were at last swung aboard.

The raid had been hard on the wounded in the wards of the ship, because of the terrible helplessness of being unable to move. The ship seemed to lie directly under a cone of ack-ack fire, and perhaps it would have been easier if the wounded had heard the German planes, so that, at least through their ears, they would know what was happening. The American medical personnel, most of whom had never been in an air raid, tranquilly continued their work, asked no questions, showed no sign even of interest in this uproar, and handed out confidence as if it were a solid thing like bread.

If anyone had come fresh to that ship in the night, someone unwounded, not attached to the ship, he would have been appalled. It began to look entirely Black-Hole-of-Calcutta, because it was airless and ill lit. Piles of bloody clothing had been cut off and dumped out of the way in corners; coffee cups and cigarette stubs littered the decks; plasma bottles hung from cords, and all the fearful surgical apparatus for holding broken bones made shadows on the walls. There were wounded who groaned in their sleep or called out and there was the soft steady hum of conversation among the wounded who could not sleep. That is the way it would have looked to anyone seeing it fresh—a ship carrying a load of pain, with everyone waiting for daylight, everyone hoping for the anchor to be raised, everyone longing for England. It was that but it was something else too; it was a safe ship no matter what happened to it. We were together and we counted on each other. We knew that from the British captain to the pink-cheeked little London mess boy every one of the ship's company did his job tirelessly and well. The wounded knew that the doctors and nurses and orderlies belonged to them utterly and would not fail them. And all of us knew that our own wounded were good men and that with their amazing help, their selflessness and self-control, we would get through all right.

The wounded looked much better in the morning. The human machine is the most delicate and rare of all, and it is obviously built to survive, if given half a chance. The ship moved steadily across the Channel and we could feel England coming nearer. Then the coast came into sight and the green of England looked quite different from the way it had looked only two days ago; it looked cooler and clearer and wonderfully safe. The beaches along this coast were only lovely yellow sand. The air of England flowed down through the wards and the wounded seemed to feel it. The sound of their voices brightened and sharpened, and they began making dates with each other for when they would be on convalescent leave in London.

We saw again the great armada of the invasion, waiting or moving out toward France. This vast directed strength seemed more like an act of nature than a thing men alone could manage. The captain shouted down from the bridge, "Look at it! By God, just look at it!"

American ambulance companies were waiting on the pier, the same efficient swift colored troops I had seen working on the piers and landing ramps before we left. On the quay there were conferences of important shore personages and our captain and the chief medical officer; and a few of us, old-timers by now, leaned over the rail and joked about being back in the paper-work department again. Everyone felt happy and you could see it in all their faces. The head nurse, smiling though gray with weariness, said, "We'll do it better next time."

As the first wounded were carried from the ship the chief medical officer, watching them, said, "Made it." That was the great thing. Now they would restock their supplies, clean the ship, cover the beds with fresh blankets, sleep whatever hours they could, and then they would go back to France. But this first trip was done; this much was to the good; they had made it.

from "Dachau"

.... Behind the barbed wire and the electric fence, the skeletons sat in the sun and searched themselves for lice. They have no age and no faces; they all look alike and like nothing you will ever see if you are lucky. We crossed the wide, crowded, dusty compound between the prison barracks and went to the hospital. In the hall sat more of the skeletons, and from them came the smell of disease and death. They watched us but did not move; no expression shows on a face that is only yellowish, stubbly skin, stretched across bone. What had been a man dragged himself into the doctor's office; he was a Pole and he was about six feet tall and he weighed less than a hundred pounds and he wore a striped prison shirt, a pair of unlaced boots, and a blanket which he tried to hold around his legs. His eyes were large and strange and stood out from his face, and his jawbone seemed to be cutting through his skin. He had come to Dachau from Buchenwald on the last death transport. There were fifty boxcars of his dead traveling companions still on the siding outside the camp, and for the last three days the American Army had forced Dachau civilians to bury these dead. When this transport had arrived, the German guards locked the men, women and children in the boxcars and there they slowly died of hunger and thirst and suffocation. They screamed and they tried to fight their way out; from time to time, the guards fired into the cars to stop the noise.

This man had survived; he was found under a pile of dead. Now he stood on the bones that were his legs and talked and suddenly he wept. "Everyone is dead," he said, and the face that was not a face twisted with pain or sorrow or horror. "No one is left. Everyone is dead. I cannot help myself. Here I am and I am finished and cannot help myself. Everyone is dead."

The Polish doctor who had been a prisoner here for five years said, "In four weeks, you will be a young man again. You will be fine."

Perhaps his body will live and take strength, but one cannot believe that his eyes will ever be like other people's eyes.

The doctor spoke with great detachment about the things he had watched in this hospital. He had watched them and there was nothing he could do to stop them. The prisoners talked in the same way—quietly, with a strange little smile as if they apologized for talking of such loathsome things to someone who lived in a real world and could hardly be expected to understand Dachau.

"The Germans made here some unusual experiments," the doctor said. "They wished to see how long an aviator could go without oxygen, how high in the sky he could go. So they had a closed car from which they pumped the oxygen. It is a quick death," he said. "It does not take more than fifteen minutes, but it is a hard death. They killed not so many people, only eight hundred in that experiment. It was found that no one can live above thirty-six thousand feet altitude without oxygen."

"Whom did they choose for this experiment?" I asked.

"Any prisoner," he said, "so long as he was healthy. They picked the strongest. The mortality was one hundred per cent, of course."

"It is very interesting, is it not?" said another Polish doctor.

We did not look at each other. I do not know how to explain it, but aside from the terrible anger you feel, you are ashamed. You are ashamed for mankind.

"There was also the experiment of the water," said the first doctor. "This was to see how long pilots could survive when they were shot down over water, like the Channel, let us say. For that, the German doctors put the prisoners in great vats and they stood in water up to their necks. It was found that the human body can resist for two and a half hours in water eight degrees below zero. They killed six hundred people in this experiment. Sometimes a man had to suffer three times, for he fainted early in the experiment, and then he was revived and a few days later the experiment was again undertaken."

"Didn't they scream, didn't they cry out?"

He smiled at that question. "There was no use in this place for a man to scream or cry out. It was no use for any man ever."....

Down the hall, in the surgery, the Polish surgeon got out the record book to look up some data on operations performed by the SS doctors. These were castration and sterilization operations. The prisoner was forced to sign a paper beforehand, saying that he willingly undertook this self-destruction. Jews and gypsies were castrated; any foreign slave laborer who had had relations with a German woman was sterilized. The German women were sent to other concentration camps.

The Polish surgeon had only his four front upper teeth left, the others on both sides having been knocked out by a guard one day, because the guard felt like breaking teeth. This act did not seem a matter of surprise to the doctor or to anyone else. No brutality could surprise them any more. They were used to a systematic cruelty that had gone on, in this concentration camp, for twelve years.

The surgeon mentioned another experiment, really a very bad one, he said, and obviously quite useless. The guinea pigs were Polish priests. (Over two thousand priests passed through Dachau; one thousand are alive.) The German doctors injected streptococci germs in the upper leg of the prisoners, between the muscle and the bone. An extensive abscess formed, accompanied by fever and extreme pain. The Polish doctor knew of more than a hundred cases treated this way; there may have been more. He had a record of thirty-one deaths, but it took usually from two to three months of ceaseless pain before the patient died, and all of them died after several operations performed during the last few days of their life. The operations were a further experiment, to see if a dying man could be saved; but the answer was that he could not. Some prisoners recovered entirely, because they were treated with the already known and proved antidote, but there were others who were now moving around the camp, as best they could, crippled for life.

Then, because I could listen to no more, my guide, a German Socialist who had been a prisoner in Dachau for ten and a half years, took me across the compound to the jail. In Dachau, if you want to rest from one horror you go and see another. The jail was a long clean building with small white cells in it. Here lived the people whom the prisoners called the N.N. N.N. stands for *Nacht und Nebel*, which means night and mist. Translated into less romantic terms, this means that the prisoners in these cells never saw a human being, were never allowed to speak to anyone, were never taken out into the sun and the air. They lived in solitary confinement on water soup and a slice of bread, which was the camp diet. There was of course the danger of going mad. But one never knew what happened to them in the years of their silence. And on the Friday before the Sunday when the Americans entered Dachau, eight thousand men were removed by the SS on a final death transport. Among these were all the prisoners from the solitary cells. None of these men has been heard of since. Now in the clean empty building a woman, alone in a cell, screamed for a long time on one terrible note, was silent for a moment, and screamed again. She had gone mad in the last few days; we came too late for her.

In Dachau if a prisoner was found with a cigarette butt in his pocket he received twenty-five to fifty lashes with a bull whip. If he failed to stand at attention with his hat off, six feet away from any SS trooper who happened to pass, he had his hands tied behind his back and he was hung by his bound hands from a hook on the wall for an hour. If he did any other little thing which displeased the jailers he was put in the box. The box is the size of a telephone booth. It is so constructed that being in it alone a man cannot sit down, or kneel down, or of course lie down. It was usual to put four men in it together. Here they stood for three days and nights without food or water or any form of sanitation. Afterward they went back to the sixteen-hour day of labor and the diet of water soup and a slice of bread like soft gray cement.

What had killed most of these people was hunger; starvation was simply routine. A man worked those incredible hours on that diet and lived in such overcrowding as cannot be imagined, the bodies packed into airless barracks, and woke each morning weaker, waiting for his death. It is not known how many people died in this camp in the twelve years of its existence, but at least forty-five thousand are known to have died in the last three years. Last February and March, two thousand were killed in the gas chamber because, though they were too weak to work, they did not have the grace to die; so it was arranged for them....

Now we were at the crematorium. "You will put a handkerchief over your nose," the guide said. There, suddenly, but never to be believed, were the bodies of the dead. They were everywhere. There were piles of them inside the oven room, but the SS had not had time to burn them. They were piled outside the door and alongside the building. They were all naked, and behind the crematorium the ragged clothing of the dead was neatly stacked, shirts, jackets, trousers, shoes, awaiting sterilization and further use. The clothing was handled with order, but the bodies were dumped like garbage, rotting in the sun, yellow and nothing but bones, bones grown huge because there was no flesh to cover them, hideous, terrible, agonizing bones, and the unendurable smell of death.

We have all seen a great deal now; we have seen too many wars and too much violent dying; we have seen hospitals, bloody and messy as butcher shops; we have seen the dead like bundles lying on all the roads of half the earth. But nowhere was there anything like this. Nothing about war was ever as insanely wicked as these starved and outraged, naked, nameless dead. Behind one pile of dead lay the clothed healthy bodies of the German soldiers who had been found in this camp. They were shot at once when the American Army entered. And for the first time anywhere one could look at a dead man with gladness.

Just behind the crematorium stood the fine big modern hothouses. Here the prisoners grew the flowers that the SS officers loved. Next to the hothouses were the vegetable gardens, and very rich ones too, where the starving prisoners cultivated the vitamin foods that kept the SS strong. But if a man, dying of hunger, furtively pulled up and gorged himself on a head of lettuce, he would be beaten until he was unconscious. In front of the crematorium, separated from it by a stretch of garden, stood a long row of well-built, commodious homes. The families of the SS officers lived here; their wives and children lived here quite happily, while the chimneys of the crematorium poured out unending smoke heavy with human ashes....

I have not talked about how it was the day the American Army arrived, though the prisoners told me. In their joy to be free, and longing to see their friends who had come at last, many prisoners rushed to the fence and died electrocuted. There were those who died cheering, because that effort of happiness was more than their bodies could endure. There were those who died because now they had food, and they ate before they could be stopped, and it killed them. I do not know words to describe the men who have survived this horror for years, three years, five years, ten years, and whose minds are as clear and unafraid as the day they entered.

I was in Dachau when the German armies surrendered unconditionally to the Allies. The same half-naked skeleton who had been dug out of the death train shuffled back into the doctor's office. He said something in Polish; his voice was no stronger than a whisper. The Polish doctor clapped his hands gently and said, "Bravo." I asked what they were talking about.

"The war is over," the doctor said. "Germany is defeated."

We sat in that room, in that accursed cemetery prison, and no one had anything more to say. Still, Dachau seemed to me the most suitable place in Europe to hear the news of victory. For surely this war was made to abolish Dachau, and all the other places like Dachau, and everything that Dachau stood for, and to abolish it forever.

—Source: "The First Hospital Ship, June 1944," "Dachau May 1945" from <u>The Face of War</u> copyright ©1988 by Martha Gellhorn. Used by permission of Grove/Atlantic, Inc.

PATRICIA LOCHRIDGE

After an apprenticeship on a small newspaper in Missouri, Patricia Lochridge, also a graduate of the Columbia School of Journalism, was hired by CBS in the late 30's to work at their New York office. After the attack on Pearl Harbor, she was employed by the Office of War Information in Washington, D.C. and later became the only woman war correspondent to report from both the European and Pacific Theaters of Operation.

When the Pacific area was finally opened to women correspondents in 1945, <u>Woman's Home Companion</u> chose to send Lochridge. She was assigned to Hawaii and Guam, and finally covered the battle for Iwo Jima from a hospital ship serving wounded servicemen. Because she worked for a magazine and not a wire service, she was able to report in detail the nightmare created by the prolonged bloody conflict and the agony and courageous spirit of the wounded. The battle for Iwo Jima raged from February 19, 1945 until March 26, and American losses totaled more than 16,000 men.

This is the story of Iwo Jima and its wounded as I saw it on ship and shore; the story of thousands of American marines who fought the toughest bloodiest battle in their history to give us a stepping stone to Tokyo. It begins on D-day plus four, a cold gray morning on Iwo. The battle should have been almost over. But in reality it was only beginning, just as the job of the hospital ship Solace was only beginning.

I stood on the windy upper deck with a group of doctors. No one spoke very much. We were filled with a terrible dread of what we must see in the next few hours. I wondered if I could take it. This would be my first experience with actual combat. A young surgeon who understood my thoughts handed me a small sealed bottle of ammonia saying, "Look, Pat, if things get too rough and you feel faint, a sniff of this will straighten you out."

We were in action as soon as the skipper, Commander E.B. Peterson, maneuvered us inside a line of battleships, cruisers, destroyers, carriers, transports and a host of smaller craft, to an anchorage within several hundred yards of black littered beach. The gangway was ordered down and our signal flag run up to announce our readiness to receive casualties.

The ship was quickly surrounded by a swarm of small boats. From beach and combat ships, each boat brought us a dozen or more seriously wounded marines. For two long days these water ambulances came and went, and came again. Rough seas made getting the wounded aboard safely a difficult problem. But it was met. The crew of the Solace had learned their difficult task well at Tarawa, Kwajalein, Saipan, Guam and Peleliu.

The first marine to be carried up made our spines tingle. His chest was swathed in stained bandages, but as his bearers maneuvered on the gangway, he half rose from the stretcher and sang out: "Hey, bub, wait a minute. Take a look at that." In the distance we could see tiny figures struggling up Mt. Suribachi, the extinct volcano which the Japs had converted into one giant pillbox. And then we saw it—an American flag on the peak, snapping in the wind. The marine lay back and smiled. "I helped put her there this morning," he said.

Less than an hour had elapsed since Japanese mortar fire had wounded the proud marine on Suribachi. Now he was safe on the Solace. A doctor quickly examined his shattered chest and ordered him taken to surgery. Fifteen seconds after he had been carried away, another stretcher lay on the deck where his had rested. The wounded came on and on. Some still had their rifles; others were naked except for their battle dressings. Most were in terrible pain. All were terribly brave.

By late afternoon we had taken aboard almost four hundred patients, to be put into bunks, given transfusions and medicines; to be cleaned up and have their dressings changed; to be fed a hot dinner with perhaps a drink of medicinal whiskey to warm them after their cold days on Iwo.

By nightfall the neat shining white wards with their double-decked bunks were almost filled. On the once spotless white decks were little piles of dirty bloodstained clothing which had been cut off the men. The stain was everywhere—a splash on the toe of my shoe, little droplets on a railing where I rested my hand. You fortify yourself against it in the operating-rooms, train yourself to ignore it on bandages, on the doctors' white gowns. But there is no getting used to it everywhere.

I went from ward to ward helping the nurses and corpsmen as best I could. At every bunk there was an empty glass to be filled. One ward decided I should have a navy rating and dubbed me Water Tender 1C which the legitimate water tenders in the engine room thought a great joke. Nurse Kay Tasker gave me my insigne, a clean arm bandage with my rate painted on in Mercurochrome.

The simple things which the ship's two chaplains and I did seemed to help. Lieutenant Commander E. P. (Father) Monckton treated every patient to a dish of ice cream; Lieutenant P.C. Adams was lavish with his cigarettes; and I diversified my water tending with innumerable cans of fruit juices. But the real work was done by the Solace's seventeen doctors, thirteen nurses and one hundred and seventy-five corpsmen. They never rested.

At day's end we put out to sea several miles to protect our patients from attack by Jap submarines or planes and to protect our blacked-out fleet from the Solace's lighted decks and spotlighted red crosses. But all through the night, as the ship rocked and pitched, the medical staff worked on.

In the surgeries the first job was to sew up abdominal wounds. Then came brain and chest operations and finally amputations. The five operating-rooms were in continual use; minor surgery was done on everything from mess tables to patients' bunks.

In the wards death was fought off with whole blood flown all the way from San Francisco for transfusions, with penicillin injections and sulfa drugs. One ward alone of sixty-eight patients used 4,250,000 units of penicillin that night.

Six men died. But three hundred and ninety-six of the worst shot-up men in the war were still alive in the morning when we returned to our post beside Iwo's crowded bloody beach.

I was clutching my bottle of ammonia in real need as the new casualties were brought aboard, until a wounded marine greeted me: "Hello, toots, where's Miss MacDonald?" he shouted. "Take me back to her old ward. She fixed me up good at Saipan and I need more of the same medicine bad."

My tightening throat relaxed before such courage and I determinedly shoved the old ammonia bottle back in my pocket. Grinning down at him, we went to find Nurse Mac. After the meeting was over, I sat on the edge of his bunk to wash a little of Iwo's grime from his face and hear news of the action.

The news was not good. This tough experienced marine had found, as had all the men, that Iwo was worse than his wildest nightmares—the impenetrable blockhouses which no artillery or bombing could knock out, the thousand-pound rockets and huge mortar shells, the lack of vegetation for cover, the raw bitter cold.

The wounded coming aboard from the beach were eagerly questioned by earlier arrivals. "Did you hear how the Fourth's doing? Were the 27th Marines relieved? Is it still bad on the beach? You didn't hear what happened to Joe, my platoon leader, did you?"

The ward hummed with men swapping stories. Only once was it still. A red-haired corporal choked out the words: "They got me when they killed John." Each man knew that John was Gunnery Sergeant John Basilone, Congressional Medal of Honor veteran of Guadalcanal, whom all marines believed invulnerable. In the stillness I couldn't bear the expression on their faces. They knew John had refused a safe billet in the United States. They thought of John Basilone's wife, a marine sergeant herself in the Women's Reserve.

During the second day the ship began to smell of blood, disinfectants, gangrene and death. I went up on deck to try to get away from it, but it followed me and in desperation I liberally doused myself with a bottle of perfumed toilet water. Afterward I stopped to talk to one of my favorite patients, a badly burned Negro sailor. He smiled through all his bandages and wrinkled up his nose: "Mmmn, mmnph, that is good gal smell." Other men seemed to recognize and appreciate what they call "foo foo water" and I quickly used up my bottle dabbing their pillows.

I wanted to go ashore to see how the navy doctors and corpsmen were operating. Although under continual heavy mortar and artillery fire, they somehow managed to patch up the wounded and give plasma.

A young sergeant heard that I was going and volunteered to lend me his luck, a pair of field boots which had carried him through five operations. Still another marine remembered that he had left his musette bag on the beach containing pictures of his family. Could I find it and bring it back?

That was an assignment I failed. The confusion ashore was incredible. All kinds of equipment and stores, some damaged and some intact, were scattered in what looked like a vast junk pile. Finding one small bag in all that wreckage was impossible. And Jap mortar shells were still coming over. Men who had been wounded were killed, or wounded again, as they waited in the casualty stations on the beach for small boats to take them to refuge on a transport or hospital ship.

When I returned, it was almost time for the Solace to leave. She was already carrying six hundred and forty patients, more than ever before in thirteen trips covering every marine amphibious action from Tarawa to Peleliu. Her orders were to return to Saipan, deliver the casualties to hospitals and start back at once for Iwo for another load.

The wards were so crowded that the less seriously wounded men were moved to cots on the ship's promenade decks. Finally the ship's crew were moved from their quarters to make even more room.

Casualties seemed to grow worse as we stayed. The doctors marveled that many lived at all. One surgeon said: "Some live and you don't know why. Others die and you don't know why either." Many had lost parts of two limbs; others were disfigured by shrapnel. But marines don't feel sorry for themselves. Their only complaint was, "Those dirty Japs got me before I fired a shot."

Of course there was one corporal who cursed the Japs pretty violently for messing up his artistic tattooing project. He had had two bluebirds on his chest and now one was totally obliterated by a shell fragment.

Another marine kept reiterating plaintively, "They got me on my birthday. Those lousy bastards, they couldn't shoot me yesterday, they couldn't shoot me tomorrow, they had to shoot me today, my twenty-first birthday."

Sickest in his mind was a tall handsome private first class who came aboard weeping as though his heart would break. I talked to Red for hours and finally he told me his story. High-ranking marine officers have enlisted men assigned to them to drive their jeeps and to act as bodyguards. For four days and nights Red had watched over his colonel, on the alert for Japs who might infiltrate during the night and kill the colonel as he slept. Red never had a moment's rest and finally his tired nerves snapped. He could not remember what had happened to the colonel or himself, but he felt he had failed in his mission. He kept asking over and over if the colonel was safe. I could not find out. All that the ship's psychiatrist could do was to give Red sleep.

Talking with an individual was difficult because everybody eavesdropped. If they thought a marine was exaggerating his own or his outfit's deeds of glory, they warned me quickly: "Look out, Pat, he's snowing you."

The gallantry of the marines was wonderful. They thanked you for nothing—a kind word, a smile, a cigarette, a glass of water.

A few of the patients, well enough to get out of bed occasionally, helped the overworked nurses and corpsmen. When a friend would call for the rose bowl, marine slang for bedpan, a corporal with a broken arm would hop out of his bunk and go to work.

A sergeant, in spite of a bad injury to his own leg, insisted upon standing beside one of his men while the doctor amputated the boy's leg. He told me later: "Old Jack thought he wouldn't be so scared if I was there."

Most of the men stood the pain too well. They literally refused to admit it. The nurses could give them something to ease it, but they would not ask.

The one thing marines cannot stand is being lied to about their condition. They are men accustomed to having the facts. When a marine asks how seriously he is hurt, he wants to know the truth. When they do know they are willing to help. One man told me: "You know I told the doc last night around midnight that I wasn't doing so good. I needed some help or I wouldn't make it. He gave me another pint of blood and I'm okay this morning."

I thought I was going to be okay too, but as I passed the resuscitation surgery which the crew nicknamed Dr. Hansen's Moratorium because some of the worst cases died there, the doctor called out, "Say, Pat, there's a guy here who says he knows you."

I went in. I didn't recognize the marine who lay so still on the operating table, his dungarees bloody and torn, his face black with Iwo's grit. Then someone gently lifted off his helmet and I saw his clipped blond head. Yes, I knew him. It was Bill, a lieutenant I'd danced with just a few short days ago at his division's farewell party on Guam.

We talked a little while Dr. Hansen started the whole blood running back into his veins and then Bill closed his eyes and seemed to sleep. Quietly the doctor let me have it. A shell fragment had severed his spinal cord. "The boy may not live. If he does he will never walk again."

A case like Bill's, or a death, blighted any exultation for me no matter how many other lives were saved. I doubly pitied the nurses, doctors and corpsmen. However hard and skillfully they fight, some must die.

I pitied most of all the ship's senior medical officer, Captain W.W. Hall. Harassed, unsleeping, he was all over the ship watching out for everything, his work seldom lightened by contact with the easier happier cases—there he was not needed—but always, for his advice and help, brought soul-deep into the difficult and heartbreaking.

Heartbreaking for him was the decision to up anchor for Saipan when he knew we must leave many wounded behind. He was standing with me on the quarter-deck as the gangway came up. We heard a wounded marine's sobbing cry from one of the ambulance boats.

"Don't go, don't go," he cried. As we started to pull away he shouted again: "If I had my rifle I'd shoot you. Come back."

But Dr. Hall had this consolation, that with Captain Peterson's help the ship would be driven to Saipan as fast as its old engines could turn, and then back once more to Iwo, bringing solace.

—Source: "Solace at Iwo," by Patricia Lockridge in <u>Woman's Home Companion</u>, Vol. 72, No. 5, May, 1945.

7

CLANDESTINE ACTIVIST

Not all American women who made contributions to the cause of freedom in World War II worked under the auspices of recognized and accepted American institutions. Some, living as American citizens on foreign soil, were caught up in the tragic immediacy of the war and developed their own avenues of resistance in countries overrun by the enemy.

One such individual, Margaret Doolin Utinsky, was working as an American Red Cross volunteer nurse in Manila in 1941 when she was ordered to board The Washington, the last ship to carry Army wives and non-vital personnel to safety; she was to leave behind her civilian engineer husband who had been ordered by the U.S. government to Bataan to help. She defied the order and remarked to Jack before his departure, "I won't be one of those thousands of women back in the States who have to sit and wonder every minute what is happening here in the Islands. What can I do over there? Here at least I could help if anything happened." The "if" became a reality when the Japanese marched into Manila on January 2, 1942.

American citizens who did not flee, now "enemy aliens," were interned in the detention camp at Santo Tomas, but Utinsky furtively hid out in her apartment. There, listening surreptitiously to the "Voice of Freedom" being broadcast from the tunnels of Corregidor, she heard the report of the fall of Bataan, then Corregidor,—then silence. Utinsky determined that she would go to Bataan to search for Jack.

With the help of Father Lalor, a local priest quietly engaged in aiding the Americans and Filipinos, Utinsky obtained papers identifying her as an unmarried nurse of Lithuanian extraction, assuming the neutrality of that country. Under this guise she was able to accompany the Red Cross on its humanitarian missions to the "liberated" Filipinos.

This is the story of Utinsky's quest for Jack and how it led her to establish a fledgling smuggling operation that later evolved into a sophisticated network involving many "helpers," from Camp O'Donnell to Cabanatuan, who at great personal peril supplied American prisoners of war with life-sustaining provisions. Many of her group were tortured; many were killed. Eventually Utinsky herself was arrested by the Japanese. After a month of detention and excruciating torture at Fort Santiago during which she revealed nothing about her operation, Utinsky's resolve and audacity never wavered. "Of course, I went straight back to smuggling again, starting the life-saving supplies moving to Cabanatuan." Perhaps her grit and determination are best summed up in the words of a grateful government who recognized her "extremely hazardous and valuable services," "her inspiring bravery and unfaltering devotion to duty" when they bestowed on her the Medal of Freedom.

MARGARET UTINSKY

The story of Utinsky's involvement with the American prisoners of war in the Philippines began when she accompanied the Red Cross on its humanitarian missions to Bataan, where her husband Jack was known to be working with the U.S. before the island fell to the Japanese. Here she records the shock of discovering the savage brutality that marked the infamous Death March.

...We came at last to the road where the March of Death had taken place. We came so soon after the surrender that the dead bodies were everywhere. There was no evidence that a battle had taken place, yet thousands had died here. Bodies lay all around, some beside the road, some in the rice paddies, some in the ditches. I was sick with shock. I could not believe my eyes.

Every foot of the way brought new horrors. I can not blot out the awful picture of starved dogs tearing at those poor bodies, running off, growling, carrying a man's hand or a whole arm, tearing at his face. The bodies had been stripped of everything of value, even shoes and identification tags. Japanese soldiers were walking around with American wrist watches strapped on their arms all the way from the wrist to the elbow.

At Abucay there was a bombed church with part of the roof intact, and we decided to put a clinic there. The natives swarmed around us and I asked them why there were so many Americans dead. Then, little by little, they told me the story of the March of Death. For five days and five nights, they said, they had heard the men screaming incessantly. They were beaten with bayonets to make them march faster. They were worn out from the long battle; most of them were sick and almost starved. But they plodded on, some of them dropping right in their tracks. When they fell, the Japanese stabbed them with bayonets and tossed them into the ditches beside the road. Sometimes they left the poor, emaciated bodies in the road and the oncoming trucks ran over them as they lay there.

I saw a spot where thirty wounded men had been tied together with barbed wire run through their hands, then thrown into a barbed wire entanglement and machine-gunned. Another group of thirteen men were so weak they could not walk. They kept falling. The Japanese wired them together with barbed wire and when one fell he dragged the others down. At length, the Japanese pushed them into an open latrine and forced their comrades, at the point of guns, to bury them alive.

Two Filipinos on that March of Death had cans of sardines hidden in their clothes. They opened them and tried to eat. The Japanese chopped off their arms, flung them into the fields, and then slashed them up, cutting them to pieces. They polluted the water and forced the Americans to drink it. As I walked the roads of the stricken area, I noticed small artesian wells that bubbled up on either side. This explained why so many men in that grim procession lay sprawled in the grotesque attitudes of sudden death just off the roads. They had been mad with thirst and had dared to step aside for a drink of water.

After this trip through filth and nightmare, when everything seemed to be festering death, I knew that I could not stop until I had given every ounce of my strength to help the men who still lived. And somewhere among them was Jack. I felt sure of that. Though I had searched and searched among those pitiful dead bodies, I had not found him.

On her second Red Cross mission to Bataan, Utinsky requested permission to become a field nurse so she could make contact with American prisoners allowed to scavenge for food outside the prison walls. It was in that capacity that she first was able to smuggle food and drugs to prisoners, though on a very limited scale. At this time she also began collecting the names of prisoners and of those who had died; this list became the core of the most complete record ever obtained by the War Department. When Utinsky began working with Dr. Atienza in Capas, near Camp O'Donnell, the smuggling of supplies to the prisoners of war began in earnest. Utinsky arrived at her post loaded with disguised packages of provisions taken from her apartment in Manila.

How great the need of the American prisoners was I did not learn until I had talked to Dr. Atienza. As a member of the Filipino Red Cross he was permitted to visit Camp O'Donnell, where he was allowed to look after the sick Filipino prisoners. They were not, of course, supposed to have any contact with the Americans or to give them any aid. But Dr. Atienza had managed to get in touch with Colonel Duckworth, Major Berry, and Chaplain Tiffany, inside the prison, and through them he was confident that he could get help to the Americans.

Our men, he said, were starving. The Japanese allowed a pittance to the soldiers, ten *centavos* (about five cents) a day, with which they had to buy their food. Officers were given twenty pesos (about ten dollars) a month. With the permission of the Japanese, the officers had pooled their money so as to provide food for all. But even this amount was cut, as a man was not paid if he was too sick or too weak from lack of food to work.

The men desperately needed food, money to buy food, drugs, clothing—and all of this would have to be smuggled in. But Dr. Atienza had discovered a way to do it. When the Filipino prisoners were released, those who were ill were brought out of the prison in ambulances or trucks to be loaded on cattle cars. These ambulances were carefully searched when they left the prison, lest someone should try to escape or blankets should be smuggled out, but no search was made when they returned to the prison.

We could hardly have asked for a better arrangement, since this meant that Dr. Atienza would be able to take in the supplies I had brought with me without any danger of having them confiscated.

Next morning, as he was preparing to pack my supplies in the ambulance, he asked suddenly, "Why don't you send in a note with these things, asking for a receipt? In that way, you may be sure that your supplies are actually reaching the American prisoners."

I agreed and wrote the note. Then I hesitated. I did not know how to sign it. If it were found, there would be trouble for everyone, and trouble in a big way for me. So after a moment's thought, I signed the note "Miss U." And with that signature, the Miss U organization came to hazy birth.

From that time on, all sorts of stories and rumors circulated about Miss U. I listened to all kinds of speculations about myself. I was Chinese. I was Russian. I was everything under the sun.

That day, Dr. Atienza came back from Camp O'Donnell bringing a receipt for the stuff I had sent in. Well, at least we knew where we stood. Dr. Atienza could smuggle the stuff in if I could get it. I knew that as long as my commissary supplies lasted, I would have food to bring them. The problem was clothing, drugs, and money.

I arranged with Dr. Atienza to go up to Capas for each release date, when Filipino prisoners were sent back to Manila. I began traveling back and forth to Capas like a commuter, each time loaded with all the food I could carry, but all I could carry was terribly little for so many men in desperate need. It did amuse me, though, to think that I was carrying it all on a Japanese railroad. There was a certain justice in that.

But food was not enough. The men needed drugs. They needed clothing. And most of all they needed money.

In any conquered city, one commodity is prized above all else—money. And I needed it badly. I went back to Manila after that first trip and looked around the apartment to find what I could sell. Before the war, my husband and I had been proud of our silver service, and of our Spode and Wedgewood china, but now it had nothing for me but a cash value. I sold the china for over $200 and the silver for $400. My rings and pearls and a bracelet, sold to a jeweler, added a lot more money to my supply. There was nothing else but my electric stove, and I heard of a couple at the opposite end of Manila who were trying to furnish a house. They were so glad to get a stove they did not quibble over my $200 price. One by one, the possessions that had given meaning to my pre-war life were passing from me, but at least I was accumulating a sizable sum with which to buy drugs and clothing for starving men.

Buy as carefully as I could, however, the money dwindled away, just as the food cache, which had seemed so inexhaustible when I had first filled the apartment, shrank smaller and smaller.

Well, if I could not buy, I could beg. I went to Father Lalor with my problems and he helped me, as he was always to help me. Day after day he walked the streets of Manila, asking everyone he could trust for old shoes. Between the two of us, we must have collected several thousand pairs, which we stored at the convent until I could get them to Camp O'Donnell.

I became a regular panhandler. I begged everywhere. In shops, in churches, in the houses of friends, in the offices of total strangers. Getting clothing and drugs and food, I told them in the beginning, for the Filipinos. There was so much to be done that I could not handle it alone, and there was always the risk of asking the wrong person for help. But I figured that unless I took risks I would get nothing done.

So I went to the people I knew best, to those I knew were loyal to the United States, and told them bluntly of the urgent and dire need of the sick and starving men at Camp O'Donnell.

They were afraid. Well, I could understand that. Live under enemy occupation long enough and you begin to breathe an air of suspicion. You don't trust your friends or your neighbors or your own relatives. And most of the time you are probably justified. But part of the hesitancy of my friends was as much for my sake as for their own. I understood that too. Not simply because they feared I would be caught by the Japanese, but because they thought I might become involved with some unscrupulous group that would be vile enough to exploit even the unfortunates in the prison camps.

"How do you know, after all," they demanded, "that the things actually reach the prisoners?"

"That's easy," I explained. "Everything that I send in has a note with it, asking for a receipt. If you get a receipt, will you believe that you have really made contact with the American prisoners? Will you help them then?"

Yes, they would believe if they got a receipt.

So I went back to Capas again and with Dr. Atienza's help smuggled the money from my furnishings and jewelry into the camp, part of it going to Chaplain Tiffany, the rest to Colonel Duckworth for the hospital. I asked the men to send out notes indicating what they had received, and telling me what they needed. Then, armed with the prisoners' notes, I went back to Manila again.

The notes turned the trick. Through Father Lalor, I was able to reach American sympathizers—Chinese, Swiss, Spanish, Filipino—whom I tapped ruthlessly, though few of them knew my identity. To most of those who helped me, except those who became a close part of the organization, I remained "Miss U," a woman whom nobody knew.

Notes from the prisoners were shown to anyone from whom we could beg a few pesos, or order food, or medical supplies. Soon the life-saving stuff was coming in to us in an ever-increasing stream. We stored it at the convent until it could be delivered. And night after night, when I had gone to bed, I allowed myself to wonder whether any of the food was reaching Jack. I had not heard a word, yet somehow I knew he was a prisoner somewhere. Risks did not seem too dangerous when I thought of him inside those fences....

We had fallen into a routine now. We collected money and supplies in Manila. We packed them, hiding the money and notes and drugs. We stored supplies at the Malate Convent. From the contact people in Capas to the contact people in the prison camp, messages and supplies must be taken and lists brought back out. Day in, day out, the game went on....

Then at four o'clock on a December morning, when I was at Capas, I was awakened by singing.

"Good-night, ladies. Good-night, ladies," drifted back to me. I knew. The prisoners were leaving Camp O'Donnell, marching off for Cabanatuan prison camp. They were going out singing.

They sang because they felt sure that whatever lay ahead would be better than what lay behind. How, they reasoned, could it be worse? Only 200 men were leaving Camp O'Donnell. In the prison graveyard lay 1700 of their comrades who could not march with them. They had died since May. Only 200 saved. Somehow, in some way, I would have to operate on a bigger scale at Cabanatuan.

I never saw the men again, but I knew I had to keep working for them and for others like them. And perhaps Jack might be where they were going.

During her first contact with the prisoners at Cabanatuan, Utinsky finally learned of Jack's fate; she also determined to continue her work, though necessarily on a larger scale, by utilizing a different method to cope with conditions at Cabanatuan.

If I was going to help the prisoners in Cabanatuan prison camp, I would have to find a new method. I could no longer use the excuse of Filipino relief, which had made it possible for me to go and come from Capas, because all the Filipino prisoners had been released....

I sent Naomi [a helper] with two Filipino boys to the little town of Cabanatuan to scout around and see what they could learn. They went as peanut vendors, hawking their peanuts near the prison gates. Naomi was the first of them to make a contact—with Colonel Mack, who was a slave laborer on a vegetable garden project near the camp....

One of the first questions Naomi asked Colonel Mack was whether Jack Utinsky was at Cabanatuan. He answered that he was going back into camp and that he would be out again that day. While he was inside, he succeeded in asking a number of men about Jack. When he met Naomi again, he slipped her a letter. "This will tell you what you asked," he said, and he went on with his work.

That night Naomi brought me the letter at the apartment.

"Dear Miss U," it read, "you have many friends in this place. It is from them that I have been able to get this story of your husband. I am deeply sorry that I have to tell you what I found out. Your husband died here on August 6, 1942. He is buried here in the prison graveyard. I know how you have tried in every way to get word about him. I am sure that this is the true story. Men here who knew him verified it.

"You will be told that he died of tuberculosis. That is not true. The men say that he actually died of starvation. A little more food and medicine, which they would not give him here, might have saved him.

"This is terrible news for you, who have, with your unselfish work, been able to save so many others. All of us will always owe you a debt that we can never pay for what you have done.

"I do want to say to you that this place is far more dangerous for your work than Camp O'Donnell was. Do not take risks that you took there. If you never do another thing, you already have done more than any living person to help our men. My sympathy goes out to you in your grief. God bless you in all you do.

Sincerely yours,

Edward Mack,
Lt. Colonel, U.S. Army

I did not cry. I was too numb for that. Naomi said the comforting things one does say at a time like that but they did not seem to make much sense. I sat there holding the letter. Jack was dead. He had starved to death. If he could have received just a little of the food I had given to others, he might be alive. If I had found him four months sooner, he might be alive....

The reason that had been the mainspring of my work was gone. But remembering that Jack could have lived if he had had food and medicine, I was determined to go on. It was more important than ever to go on....

The size of the job appalled me. There had been 1700 prisoners at Camp O'Donnell. At Cabanatuan there were more than 9000 men. It was a mountainous task, and if these prisoners were to be kept alive, my operations would have to be speeded up and handled on a far greater scale than I had ever contemplated at O'Donnell. Well, there was no point in being scared before I even got started. The idea was to make a beginning of some sort.

Up to now I had been working on a permit which allowed me to travel back and forth to Capas to help with the Filipino releases. I needed a new kind of permit, "for the needy of Cabanatuan." Mrs. Kummer arranged it for me, and the Japanese interpreted the "needy of Cabanatuan" as the Filipinos of the district, which is what I meant them to do.

At Camp O'Donnell we had smuggled our supplies into the prison in empty trucks and ambulances. The situation at Cabanatuan was different. There was no question of our getting anything into the prison here. As Colonel Mack had pointed out, this was a lot more dangerous than our activities at O'Donnell had been. Our job, therefore, was to contact the Americans when they came out of the prison and get our supplies to them directly.

Every day about a thousand prisoners went out to work on the farm where they raised vegetables for the Japanese. When they came out, the guards would allow them to spend their pay by buying from the native vendors who circulated among them with baskets on their heads. Then, several times a week, the prisoners came out with bullcarts, pulled by *carabao* to buy what vegetables and fruits they could at the stalls.

Of course, before the men could buy anything at the stalls they had to have money, so Naomi and Evangeline Neibert, dressed as vendors, with baskets on their heads, went about with sacks of roasted peanuts. They sold these sacks to the prisoners for a centavo, and in each package of peanuts we hid money, as much as two or three hundred pesos, which was possible because all the money was paper and could be rolled up.

It worked like this. A prisoner would come up to a vendor, buy a sack of peanuts for a peso, get back a ten-peso note as change and a bag of peanuts containing a lot more pesos.

This was not a drop in the bucket compared with the needs of the camp. We had to find a way of getting quantities of food to the men. We needed a truck to ship the stuff in, and we needed some place at Cabanatuan where we could dispose of it to the prisoners without arousing the suspicion of the Japanese, who guarded them every minute. It seemed like a tall order, but we managed it.

One of the Filipino dealers at Cabanatuan was a man named Maluto who had a number of stalls in the market there. One day Naomi stopped to talk to him. To approach anyone and ask for help with our work was the most dangerous thing we had to do. Not only the safety of the individual but also the safety of the group was at stake every time a contact was made. For if we made a mistake and struck a collaborationist, that would be the end.

The Japanese had killed Maluto's son and he was no collaborationist. He was heart and soul for the Americans....

Maluto was afraid and he didn't pretend otherwise. But he took my address...listened to my story and he promised to help. Yes, he would let us use his stalls for smuggled goods for the Americans.

Now the problem was to get the supplies....

The need for food and drugs and clothing and—above all—for money was more desperate than it had been before. The conditions under which the men lived were horrible, they were starving and many of them were hospital cases. To get anything, there had to be money. As time went on, I discovered that people who were hesitant or even indifferent about providing money for unknown men would be most helpful if they knew the person whom they were aiding. There was something real and immediate about the hunger of a particular John Smith; an unidentified soldier was hunger in the abstract.

So I sent word that the prisoners were to give us the names of anyone whom they might know in Manila. Lt. Colonel Mack talked to them and asked them to send me any names they could. "But don't waste time thinking about casual acquaintances," he warned them. "Mind, only those you can trust."

One by one, after that, names would be forwarded to me. I never hesitated in approaching these people. They were both rich and poor, and not one ever failed to give me as much as he or she could in money or food. And never was I betrayed. In all my recruiting of volunteer help, indeed, I never met a single fifth-columnist through people whose names were sent me by prisoners in the camp.

Each time I asked for little in the beginning. "Wait for a receipt," I said, "and then you can be sure that your friend actually received what you sent him." When they got the receipts they began to contribute regularly. Each prisoner so provided for meant that there were fewer to draw on the main kitty. And yet there were still so terribly many!

The garage of the Malate Convent was a convenient storehouse. No suspicion was aroused by loads of supplies leaving there, for the Irish priests had a whole countryside, naked and starving, for which they felt responsible.

After a while I began getting so many supplies that it was no longer possible to carry them piecemeal by train. And again, when the need arose, we found the means to meet it. A wealthy polo player, Juan Elizalde, owner of a distillery, gave me the use of a truck and alcohol to replace gasoline as motor fuel....

Again, as at Camp O'Donnell, the almost childish simplicity of our arrangements was their guarantee of success. Several times a week, our truck went back and forth from the convent to Maluto's stalls at Cabanatuan, and the same system of code messages employed at O'Donnell was used.

With the truck I could send quite large shipments to the camp area. There were no difficulties. Our Filipino drivers were within the law. There was little restriction on their moving about. And doctors and nurses were privileged under Red Cross to give relief. So we were able to keep moving without arousing too much comment. The truck was loaded with sweet potatoes, drugs, canned foods, mongo beans—the latter a superlative preventative and treatment for beriberi.

The day our shipment was made, one of our workers at Cabanatuan would get word to the prisoners that it was coming and describe what we were sending. That day the Americans would present the Japanese commandant with a list of items they wanted to buy in the market. The list always tallied with what we had for them. If I sent in clothes, they said that was what they needed. Obviously this list could not cover more items than might be purchased with the money they obtained from their "Geneva Convention wages." After seeing that the list and the money tallied, the commandant would sign the statement and the Yanks drove their carts off to market.

Of course, they never went to Maluto's stalls first. But after inspecting the vegetables on sale at the other stalls they would come to my friend. There would be a great haggling over price, under the watchful eye of their Japanese guards, then a deal would be made. All of the items on the list would be loaded into the carts. But in addition there would be all the food and medicine that I had sent to Maluto's stalls. Back to camp would go the carts. The first man in the procession would present the list with the commandant's signature. The sentry would examine it. Within half an hour my food and medicine would be doing their job.

What happened, of course, was that everything they "purchased" at Maluto's stalls they really got for free. Then they had their money to buy extra food and perishables that I could not ship them at the other stalls. And always, among the sacks they acquired at Maluto's stalls, there would be one that was marked with red lettering, which was taken to our head contact man in the prison. This sack was filled with pesos and a note indicating which men were to receive the money, and how much was intended for each one. The money would then be distributed inside the prison.

As was inevitable with our activities on so big a scale, the little town of Cabanatuan was aware of the work that was being done. Pretty soon almost everyone in town was either working for me or wanting to work for me. There were a few, of course, who collaborated with the Japanese. That was true everywhere. But we soon learned who they were and so we could be on our guard against them. The other people in town would look after them for us.

Narrow escapes were the order of the day at Cabanatuan.... If the Americans were to be kept alive—if any of them were to be kept alive under the starvation regime on which the Japanese were keeping them—risks had to be taken....

So it went on. Then it became apparent that even the truckloads of food and drugs were not enough for the camp. Some way had to be found to increase the amount of provisions that I could get to the men. That way, too, was provided.

Maluto had arranged to rent a boxcar from the Japanese in which he shipped supplies from his Manila warehouses to his stalls in Cabanatuan. I asked him to rent a second boxcar to carry my stuff....

...By this fast method of shipment we were even able to send such perishables as green vegetables and fresh fruit which the men needed. All my workers, of course, dressed like Filipinos and they loaded the boxcar without any trouble.

Each large sack of vegetables would contain somewhere in the midst of its contents of red beans or *mongo* beans or camotes, packages marked with a sign or numeral. Lieutenant Colonel Mack would have lists which had gone ahead by runner with the name of the man for whom the package had been prepared opposite the sign. There was never a slip-up. These packages might contain anything. We answered every single request we humanly could from the prisoners, even having false teeth repaired which had been broken when the Japanese were beating the prisoners.

The amazing part of the thing was that our boxcar traveled up and down on the Japanese railroad right under the noses of Japanese guards in the stations, along the route and at both terminals. Never was there any interference with that enormous flow of food and drugs. It seemed like a far cry from those days at Camp O'Donnell when I traveled to Capas [on the train], surrounded by my motley array of bundles, crying Filipino babies, and squawking chickens. Then I had worked practically alone. Now I had more than a score of workers and a smoothly running organization. It was to cost something in pain and in lives, but that was not yet....

Members of Utinsky's operation began to be apprehended for questioning. Despite being tortured, no one revealed details of the group's activities. But "Miss U" knew that she was being watched and that arrest was unavoidable. As she says, "Sooner or later I knew the Japanese would get me. They were bound to."

It was on the morning of Friday, September 28, that I set out for the hospital.... As I left the house I knew that I was being watched. The hospital too was under surveillance. It is unpleasant to walk deliberately into a trap.

It was about eleven o'clock in the morning, and I was looking after one of my patients, a woman named Zenia Jastin, who was ill with cancer, when it happened. The tramp of heavy feet in the corridor coming toward the ward where I was. I stiffened up. They were at the door, eight of them, fully armed, bayonets fixed.

"You will come," one of them said, and I went. The eight Japanese fell into formation around me and we marched down the hall and out of the building. I was grateful now for the dark glasses which I had taken to wearing ever since I had become a Lithuanian. If I was going to make a practice of telling lies, I wanted something to hide my eyes, which are always a dead give-away when one is frightened. I had been wearing the things for months and right now they gave me a curious sense of protection.

I didn't know where they were taking me but it was probably Fort Santiago. That was where people usually went to be questioned. They always came out looking the worse for wear....

The Japanese soldiers took me into a large sunny room on the second floor.... Seated at a table was a Japanese officer, his saber at his side. Across the table was a younger Japanese, who was the interpreter.... The interpreter told me to sit down at the end of the table. I did as I was told. Then he ordered me to put my hands on the table, palms down, arms straight out. It was a strained, uncomfortable position that made me feel very helpless. My heart was pounding thickly at the base of my throat, and I swallowed. I wanted my voice to be steady. Whatever happened, I swore to myself, I would never give them any satisfaction by showing fear or by screaming. The first part of the vow I kept; there were a few times, later on, when I broke the second part. You can stand only so much pain.

The interpreter sat at my left. The officer with the saber sat across from me. Before them was a stack of large square papers. It didn't seem possible that anyone could have collected that much information about me. "You will swear before your God," the interpreter said, "to tell the truth."

My mouth felt like cotton. "Yes, I will swear," I said.

"The Japanese very smart people," he said. "They cannot be fooled. You better not lie. We can tell."

"I wouldn't dream of trying to fool you," I protested. "Why should I?"

"We know American and Englishmen are easy on women," he went on. "Japanese are not. If you lie to us, you will be tortured just like a man."

I had no reason to think he was bluffing.

Then, to my surprise, the two men got up and left the room. After awhile a Japanese boy came in with food: rice and fish about six inches long, officers' rations. I thought of the condemned man who ate a hearty breakfast but I could not swallow. I did change my position though and rubbed my arms to get the circulation back in them.

The two men returned, the officer's saber rattling as he sat down. My skin tightened. It was going to begin now.

"You did not eat chow," the interpreter said.

"No, I ate just before I came. I'm not hungry."

Then the questions began. *Where was I born? When?* I was Rosena Utinsky, a Lithuanian citizen, born in Kovno. I had the proper papers, thanks to Elizabeth Kummer, which I showed them.

Where was my apartment key? I gave it to them. *Where was my maid?* So they had been to the apartment that morning and found it empty. I knew darned well there was nothing incriminating for them to find there. Yet they set importance on queer things. When the huge search party had gone through my apartment [previously] they had taken away some menu cards from nightclubs and famous restaurants which I had visited on my trip to the States in 1940. There had not seemed to be much point in it and I had been amused to think they took the menu cards and overlooked three thousand pesos I had hidden, ready to smuggle to Cabanatuan.

Did my maid go to church every day? What time did she come home at night? Between questions the two men talked rapidly to each other in Japanese. There seemed to be some sharp differences of opinion between them, and from behind the dark glass I watched, trying to get some clues to the questions that were coming, some hints as to their thoughts from the sound of the words which had no meaning for me. I sat with my arms stretched out. The muscles in the upper arms and at the base of my neck were beginning to jump with fatigue.

Here it comes. *When was I in the United States?* In 1940. *Why?* For a vacation. *On what boat did I go?* This was a tricky one. I could not tell the truth because I had gone on the *Grant*, which was an Army transport. The *President Hayes,* I told them, and prayed fervently that there were no records of the *Grant's* passenger list. What *was* in that stack of papers they kept shuffling?

Better not let my attention wander. You can't slip up on the details. It's the details that catch you every time. It's the little things you have to watch.

What day did I reach America? Did they have a record of sailing and arrival dates in that stack of papers? If they did, I was sunk. I'd better tell the truth whenever I could. There had to be some guideposts of truth to cling to. Well, here goes.

"I arrived on June twenty-second."

Where? San Francisco. *Why?* I wanted to see the exposition. *Then where?* Treasure Island. *Why?* To see it. *Then where?* One thing I know they have in that stack of papers. The menu cards. They are trying to check my itinerary from them.

Before I could reorganize that trip in my mind they changed tack. *Why do you wear dark glasses? Do you need them?* I had to have them. I had a lot of trouble with my eyes and the light bothered them. *Then why did I have plain glasses too? Certainly I didn't need both pairs.* I figured that I would not be doing much reading at Fort Santiago, but I'd be doing a lot of talking. I'd hang on to the dark glasses. So they took the other pair. Then they took my shoes and the bobby pins from my hair. I was wearing a tiny gold cross hung around my neck by a fine little chain. When they reached for it, I drew back.

"Must you take that?" I asked." I've never had it off."

The interpreter snatched at it, ripping it from my neck. "Might swallow and die," he explained.

They switched back to my visit to the States. *Then where you go?* To San Antonio. *When you get there?* The Fourth of July.

That did it! The officer jumped from his chair, purple with rage, the veins in his forehead distended, and struck me full in the face with his fist. The blow knocked me out of the chair. I think it must have been then, that very first day, that they broke my jaw.

I fell sidewise, a bit behind the chair, and lay there in abject terror, seeing the officer's hand close on the hilt of the saber. I had seen enough beheadings to know what these men were capable of doing. I didn't dare move.

The interpreter stood waiting. Finally the officer said, "*Kura! Kura!*" an almost untranslatable word that means everything from "all right" to "let's get going." Painfully I pulled myself up and for good measure the officer kicked me as I rose. My mouth was full of blood and broken teeth. I spat them out on the floor.

I hope I never hear anything again about the stoical Oriental. At the slightest excitement, the Japanese begin to scream. Already the room that had been so quiet was a seething commotion. The officer was screaming at me. The spectators in the hallway were jabbering...

"Why you say Fourth July?" the officer yelled. "Big American feast day." So he did know English, after all.

I sat down again, my arms stretched out in front of me. I was shaking and could not control it. "You told me to speak the truth," I said as quietly as I could manage. "I am. That was the day I arrived in San Antonio. I don't know about the feast day. I just decided to go there and that's the day I arrived".

Why you go there? I couldn't mention relatives. Like a flash I remembered some big advertising posters. There was a rodeo there, I said quickly. I had never seen a rodeo. *What is a rodeo?* I tried to explain, pantomiming the movements of a rider on a bronch. Then one of the bystanders said brightly, "Yes, yes, rodeo. I know. Cow fight."

I embroidered on my description of a rodeo as long as I could. It was gaining me a little time until I could steady my nerves again and be ready for more questions. My cheek ached from the blow and it was beginning to swell. The pain kept distracting my attention from the questions.

Where did I go next? Chicago. *Why?* Well, my aunt in Canada went there once and told me so much about the lake and the buildings and the drive that I wanted to see them too. *Why hadn't I gone to Canada instead? I grew up there, didn't I? Then why did I go to the United States?* Because there was so little time. I already knew Canada. I wanted to see new places with what money I had.

Where did I stay in Chicago? The Y.W.C.A. It was cheaper and would give me more money for sightseeing.

Then where? New York. I seemed to be spending a lot of money for a nurse on vacation so I stressed my economies. I had taken a bus to the fair because it was cheaper than a cab. My jaw was throbbing like mad. It didn't seem possible one blow could hurt in so many different ways, mouth and gums and teeth, all with separate aches.

"You went to America on an American passport," the interpreter said.

What the deuce could be in that stack of papers anyhow? "Oh, no," I said. "I traveled on an immigration card." Someone had once described the process to me and I passed it on to the Japanese. I told them glibly about the yellow card I was given. I told them how we foreign passengers were lined up, Russians, French and I was the only Lithuanian. We signed our names in a book, I said, and then we were given a card and told we could stay for six months, but we must report to the Immigration Office every so often.

They went back to Canada again. *Why haven't I gone there?* I remembered how Naomi had been slapped for answering the same question in different words, so I was careful to repeat myself when I explained again about my aunt's visit to Chicago. And I explained it again. And again.

"You go to New York to see Fair? You are American."

There were a lot of Japanese looking at the fair, I told them, and they certainly weren't Americans. This was the first flash of spirit I had shown and every second I expected that fist to crunch into my face again, or the officer's fingers to tighten over his saber. I was almost dead from the strain of holding out my arms, from my sore mouth and jaw. At least, that is what I thought then. Later on I learned what real pain is like.

Now they were asking why I came back to the Philippines. Up to now, whenever I had found an answer I was sure of, an answer that I knew could not be contradicted by anything they might have in those papers-what in the hell was in those papers?-I had expanded on it, to give me a breathing space. Then I saw that they were encouraging me to talk on. I'd better watch out. You don't get into trouble for talking too little. You get into trouble for talking too much.

Why you leave America when you have such a good time? As a Lithuanian, I pointed out, I was practically German. War was coming. The Americans would put me in an internment camp. Anyhow, I knew no one in America. My friends were here. My work was here. *What boat you come back on?* It was a Maru boat, I said. That was logical enough. Every Japanese boat of any size was a Maru boat. A sick woman advertised she was traveling to the Orient and wanted a nurse for the voyage. I applied for the job so my passage would be paid. They took me because I did not expect to return to the States and they would have to pay my passage only one way.

Where was she going? Hongkong. Whoops, that did it! I saw the Japanese exchange a glance and remembered that Maru boats went only to Honolulu at that time. We changed at Honolulu, of course, I explained hastily, for a boat to take us on to Hongkong. *What boat?* The *Saurholt*. They didn't say anything. The old lady died in Hongkong, I went on, and I had come back to Manila.

Better be careful here. This is where the story is thin. There were no records of my arrival in Manila. I had to account for that in some way. Then I remembered hearing that the British boat *Anhue* had put in at Manila on December 8, 1941, and then had sailed without warning. The British consul had got word of the bombing of Pearl Harbor and ordered the boat out so fast that it left behind no record of its passengers, many of whom, indeed, had been stranded by that unscheduled sailing.

I described how I had tried to get hold of my papers but that I had not worried about it because it never occurred to me that anyone would want any record of my being on the boat.

They veered around again. *Tell about my father.* He died when I was a little girl. *What was my mother's name?* I invented one. *I was Lithuanian, wasn't I? Then why didn't I speak Lithuanian?* Once more I repeated the story of my childhood which had come to seem almost as real to me as the one I had actually lived. My aunt had taken me to live with her in Canada when I was very small. We always spoke English because my aunt was English.

"We know you American. We put you in Santo Tomas."

"Fine," I retorted. "Then I won't have to earn my living any more."

The two Japanese leaned back and lighted cigarettes and I tried to relax a little. The sunlight was not so bright now. There were shadows stretching toward the east. It had been a very long day.

The interpreter began to stack the papers neatly together. Were they through with me? The officer rose, then the interpreter. I dared not move.

"Get up! We go now." They beckoned to a guard. I got up stiffly. My arms tingled as I let them drop to my side. My jaw throbbed. There was dried blood on my mouth. My gums, where the teeth had been broken, were sore and swollen. My bare feet made almost no sound as I went through the doorway with the guard...

We went along a hall, down the stairs, across the patio, through the arches, and down a narrow corridor. They pushed me into a cell and the door clanged shut.

◆   ◆   ◆

It was the fifth day I remember best because that was the day the torture started. As soon as I got inside the room that morning, I knew I was in for it. The interpreter was looking too happy to suit me. I had learned a long time before that when the Japanese look happy it was a bad sign for the rest of us. And there, right on top of the pile of papers I saw my Red Cross application for volunteer work, the application which I had signed, in October, 1941, as an American!

There was only one way they could have gotten it-through the Red Cross itself. And that, I knew in a flash, meant the Filipino doctor who had turned me in to the officials during that second trip to Bataan.

The officer motioned for me to sit down. I was so scared I could hardly move but I sat down, thinking frantically, making up and discarding one story after another. This would have to be good. I had to come through this or I would never leave Fort Santiago.

The interpreter wasted no time. He tossed the paper in front of me. *You write that?* I still had no story. I leaned over, peering at it, playing for time.

"I can't see very well. Let me take it close to the window."

I held it gripped tightly as I walked slowly to the window, hoping my hands would not shake and rattle the paper. I held it up to the light and read it, word by word. Then I nodded my head. I could see both of them expand with satisfaction.

"Yes, I wrote it," I said, "but it wasn't true. I'm not an American. I told you the truth about where I was born but I lied to the Red Cross. I was afraid they wouldn't let me work for them if they knew I was a foreigner."

The officer made a gesture and the interpreter got up and pushed a bench near the table. He pointed to it.

My heart turned over as I looked at it. But there were no wires attached. That was something. I had heard about the electric machines the Japanese used for torture here, unspeakable torture. There was an electrode shaped like a curling iron which was applied to women. They would be stripped naked and forced to lie on the floor on top of wet sacks. A Japanese would stand on the woman's stomach, the electrode was thrust up the vagina and the current turned on. The agony was beyond any words. The wet sacks made a perfect conductor and the woman flung her legs and arms around madly in her suffering. One of these women was taken out of Fort Santiago in a strait jacket and sent to Santo Tomas. She was in the psychopathic ward there and finally taken to an asylum for the hopelessly insane. Another victim, who had been raped before the torture, was insane for awhile and later seemed to be nearly normal. But during the shelling of Manila, she lapsed back into a raving delirium from which she never recovered.

But this was just a bench. Its only unusual feature was that it had thin split bamboo across it for a seat—and split bamboo is as sharp as knives! I pulled down my skirt and sat down easily, carefully.

"No, no," the interpreter said. "Kneel on it."

My skirt didn't help much, though it did protect my knees a little. I let myself down gingerly on my bare shins, and leaned forward to rest my weight on my arms on the table.

The interpreter pushed them off. "Sit back," he ordered. "Sit back."

So I sat back on my heels, the bamboo cutting into my legs. That day they really went to work on me. The Red Cross application was the first concrete proof they had found that I was an American. They screamed at me. They tried to tangle me up in questions. They went back to my frequent trips to Camp O'Donnell and Cabanatuan. They said over and over that I was an American. And the officer kept slapping me.

It went on for hours, the sharp edges of the bamboo cutting deeper and deeper into my legs. The bone is close to the surface of shins. The muscles in my hips and thighs cramped and ached. The questions drilled on and on. And the officer walked around and around the bench, looking to see whether I had found a position that would keep my legs from hurting. Because I hadn't, that made him mad too, and he slapped me over and over. But I was in so much pain every other way, with my legs bleeding, my muscles cramped, that a slap more or less hardly counted.

Only now and then, when they would abruptly stop questioning me and lean back for a leisurely smoke, did I try to shift my weight from one leg to the other to ease the pain a little.

At length they said, "Get up."

I tried but I could not move my legs.

They started to shout and scream again. "Get up!"

This time I managed to move but I could not get up. I tumbled over on the floor. Pressure on the blood vessels from holding that one position so long had cut off circulation to my legs and feet. The officer stood yelling. I struggled for awhile before I could straighten out. At last I could get up, then I could stand, then I could walk.

My lacerated legs hurt worse now that circulation was restored. The thought of the *lugao* [rice] made me sick. I stumbled back to my cell. Sometime, I thought, I would have to eat more to keep up my strength—but not tonight. All I could do was lie on the floor and try to protect my cut legs from the dirt. That night I was in so much pain I almost forgot that I had beaten them again. They had not found a loophole in my story yet or they would never have let me go.

The next day we didn't go to the sunny room overlooking the patio. Instead, they took me upstairs to a long room with a piano. It must have been a sort of recreation room, but not for me. They had decided to try something else. They tied my hands behind my back, attached a rope to the tied wrists and jerked me up several feet above the floor. While I hung there, they screamed questions at me again and again and beat me with their fists.

That was the beginning of days of alternate tortures. One day would be the bamboo bench, the next day a beating. My legs never healed. And my back was a mess. They got tired of using their fists and began to beat me with the flat side of a bayonet, then with a leather belt that cut across my back.

The legs got worse. It wasn't just the bamboo. When they let me down from the beatings, they would lower me to about two feet from the floor and then drop me. Instinctively my knees would draw up and I would fall on the torn flesh. The first few times I thought the fall would kill me, but I lived through thirty-two days. And sometimes, just for variety, when his cigarette was burning brightly, the officer ground the burning coal into my arm.

All that time, all those days and days, I never screamed. I let them go ahead and do what they liked to me and didn't make a sound. But toward the end, when my shins were a mass of running sores, they took a stick, and scraped the sores. I yelled then.

One day, after I had been hanging by my wrists practically the whole day long—it is simple to say, it is harder to imagine; your arms are tied behind you, they pull you up with your weight on your twisted arms; the questions hammer on and on; without warning, at any minute, the belt comes lashing across your back, you jerk on the end of the rope; well, that's how that day was—the officer who had been torturing me took me back to my cell. I staggered on the staircase, and he said quickly, solicitously, "Be careful. You might hurt yourself."

After a total of 34 days of interrogation and torture and a period of confinement in solitary, the Japanese officers released "Rosena" Utinsky.

...on the fourth day [of solitary confinement], the door opened. All my old fears swarmed back. What now? The prison yard and a firing squad?

We were going back the way we had come. At least, it wasn't the graveyard. Whatever lay ahead, I was grateful in every inch of my body, in every part of my mind and heart, that I was walking again, that I was free of those clammy gray walls, of the iron door, of the roaches that slapped into my face, or squashed with a nauseating sound under my bare feet. But what now?

They took me to a different room this time. There were new officers and a new interpreter who asked me if I was willing to a sign a paper pledging myself never to do anything against the Japanese Government. I said yes.

"Then," he said, "I have good news for you. This officer is to give you your freedom." The officer grinned like a billy goat.

They handed me a paper and I signed it. One sentence I still remember: "Since I have been in Fort Santiago for questioning, I have received courteous treatment from all officers and sentries and been provided with good food."

Utinsky spent the next six weeks in the hospital; most of the days were filled with pain and with doubt about the final outcome of her condition. But two factors, a message from Cabanatuan and her own stolid determination, sustained her.

A message reached me in the hospital which did a lot to hearten me. It told how, in Cabanatuan, Colonel Mack, hearing of my imprisonment at Fort Santiago, had asked 6,000 Americans to pause in silent prayer for me each day. Even gangrene seemed worthwhile then.

Of course, I went straight back to smuggling again, starting the life-saving supplies moving to Cabanatuan...

Later, when Utinsky received word from Father Lalor that she was once again to be arrested, she fled Manila and joined the guerrillas fighting the Japanese from the hills of Luzon, where she remained, nursing the wounded, until the island was liberated by the Americans.

On October 17, 1946, Margaret Utinsky received the citation for the Medal of Freedom she would later be awarded for her work from May, 1942 until March, 1945, "saving hundreds of American lives."

"Mrs. Margaret Utinsky, United States citizen, serving in a civilian capacity with the United States Army. For meritorious service which has aided the United States in the prosecution of the war against the enemy on Luzon, Philippine Islands, from May 1942 to March 1945. As a leader of the "Miss U" group, Luzon Guerilla Army Forces, United States Army Forces in the Far East, Mrs. Utinsky displayed outstanding heroism and fortitude in organizing missions which alleviated the bitter suffering of American Prisoners of War. Rendering extremely hazardous and valuable services, she resourcefully collected food and medicine from Manila civilians which she surreptitiously smuggled into prison camps, thereby saving hundreds of American lives. She was captured and tortured by the Japanese, but later valiantly returned to continue her merciful work until Manila was retaken by the Americans. Through her inspiring bravery and unfaltering devotion to duty, Mrs. Utinsky made a noteworthy contribution to the effectiveness of guerrilla warfare in the Philippine Islands."

—Source: "Miss U" by Margaret Utinsky, Naylor Company, 1948.

EPILOGUE

During World War II, an unprecedented call came for women in large numbers to cross the threshold from family and household affairs to responsibilities previously considered "men's work." Although millions of American men left their jobs to serve in the military, their sacrifices were not enough. The armed forces needed more personnel. Peace time factories had to be expanded to produce increasingly larger orders for military aircraft, ships, and munitions. Civilian trades and services had to be maintained.

Men's and women's places in society were well defined and culturally accepted by most Americans at the time. Yet women from all walks of life left the relative security and comfort of their respective spheres to face an unfamiliar world in answer to their country's need. They responded with great resolve and dedication, without self-pity or the desire for self-acclaim. They embarked on enterprises and adventures seldom if ever undertaken by American women.

The accounts written by these women about their experiences at the time give us a window into a history that is unique. We learn that they were a vital component in the massive struggle to halt the aggression and cruelty taking place across the globe. They overcame whatever uncertainties and obstacles they faced and met the challenges with courage, endurance, and humor. The stories of the women of *Her War* comprise a verbal quilt of American women's significant contributions during World War II.

0-595-30373-0

Printed in the United States
23582LVS00005B/378